transforming
GRACE

transforming
GRACE

a study of 2 Corinthians

MICHAEL B. THOMPSON

The Bible Reading Fellowship
OPENING THE BIBLE

Text copyright © 1998 Michael B. Thompson

The author asserts the moral right to be
identified as the author of this work

Published by
The Bible Reading Fellowship
Peter's Way, Sandy Lane West
Oxford OX4 5HG
ISBN 1 84101 000 6

First edition 1998
10 9 8 7 6 5 4 3 2 1 0

Acknowledgments

The New Revised Standard Version of the Bible, copyright ©
1989 by the Division of Christian Education of the
National Council of the Churches of Christ in the
USA.

The Holy Bible, New International Version, copyright ©
1973, 1978, 1984 by International Bible Society.

A catalogue record for this book is
available from the British Library

Printed and bound in Great Britain
by Caledonian Book Manufacturing International,
Glasgow

FOREWORD

No book in the New Testament gives more insight into the patterns of Christian ministry than 2 Corinthians. As Michael Thompson rightly says, it 'takes us deep into the heart of Paul, and gives us his most personal message'. For that reason, amongst others, the 850 bishops coming to the Lambeth Conference, along with their spouses, will be focusing on it as they meet day by day in their groups together.

These are men and women who know, as Paul did, the ups and downs of Christian ministry and the joys and sorrows it brings, and by meeting together to look at 2 Corinthians they will, I am sure, find a great deal in common with their own experience. Indeed, one of the highlights of the 1988 Conference was these small groups and the insights they gave into being part of a worldwide Church. There is nothing like seeing the rampant consumerism of our own society through the eyes of someone whose spiritual riches are plain to see, and yet who faces physical starvation and poverty in their own country, to bring into question the values of so much that surrounds us.

Yet this is not a letter written to bishops, or even to the clergy. Christian ministry is far too important to be left to a particular group within the Church—rather, it belongs to us all. My hope is that many will use *Transforming Grace* to travel the same paths that those of us attending the Conference will be treading, and then to apply the lessons they learn to their lives and the Christian communities of which they are a part.

Michael Thompson's study guide will, I hope, enable many groups and individuals to do this, and I warmly commend it for personal and congregational use both in this country and throughout the wider Communion.

† George Cantuar

Archbishop of Canterbury

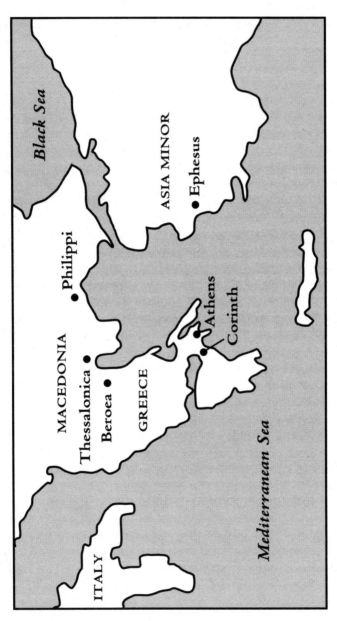

The Mediterranean in the time of Paul

6

INTRODUCTION

The purpose of this book

2 Corinthians is a fascinating letter. It takes us deep into the heart of Paul, and gives us his most personal message. In it we hear him run the gamut of emotions from ecstasy to depression, from joy to anger. We find him describing the shape of his ministry and revealing what makes him tick. We watch him work in crisis with a congregation surprisingly similar in some ways, perhaps, to our own.

However, because of its complexity, 2 Corinthians is not an easy letter to interpret; hence the need for this book. *Transforming Grace* aims to provide helpful notes and questions for thought for individuals and groups who wish to study the letter in detail. It offers a programme for six weeks of daily readings, but the material can be adapted to a shorter or longer period of study. This book is not intended to form a full commentary, since space permits no exploration of alternative explanations.

Note for use

Readers may find it helpful to read the scripture passage for the day once or twice before reading the notes, and then once again afterwards. They may then want to focus on one or two of the 'Questions for thought' given at the end of each section, rather than attempting to answer them all every day. Group leaders should be aware that some of the questions are more appropriate for private reflection than for group discussion.

The base text assumed for the readings is the *New Revised Standard Version* (NRSV), although it is not essential that the reader have that translation at hand. I have attempted throughout to help the reader understand Paul's thought by drawing out insights from the original Greek. At the risk of being too technical, occasionally I refer to the Septuagint (the

Greek translation of the Hebrew Old Testament, which Paul would have known and used). Some will want to skip the references to Greek words; the most important thing is to read and ponder the Bible itself.

Corinth and its people

Refounded by Julius Caesar in 44BC as a Roman colony after lying in ruins for more than a century, the Corinth of Paul's day was young, thoroughly modern, and impressive. Ideally situated as a crossroad for trade (see the map on page 6), it quickly became a centre for commercial traffic between Italy and Asia, and between northern and southern Greece. With trade came wealth. Large numbers of freedmen (ex-slaves) settled in Corinth to make their fortunes and to enjoy its vices. By the time Paul first visited this seaport in AD50, Corinth had become renowned for its dazzling buildings, affluence, and sexual licence. A cosmopolitan boomtown with shallow roots, Corinth was something like New York, Los Angeles and Las Vegas all rolled into one!

The values of the Corinthians sound surprisingly contemporary. The freedmen competed with each other for market share and for attention in the pursuit of upward mobility. In the absence of nobility or aristocracy because of the city's youth, power and recognition did not come through inheritance, but by self-assertion, and by flaunting one's money. *Individualism* and *image* marked Corinthian society. People used their wealth to advertise their virtue and to build their reputation in a competition for honour. Corinth's citizens were famous for their proud boasting; the florid style of Corinthian columns in architecture is a lasting testimony to their fascination with self-display. To the Corinthians, the notion of 'service' was servile. What they sought in religion was eloquence, entertainment and dramatic displays of power, not transformation and a changed life.

Paul's contacts
with the Corinthians

Paul first visited Corinth on his second missionary journey (Acts 18:1–18). He spent more than a year and a half there (Acts 18:11, 18) but, despite his investment of time, the Corinthian church remained very immature and had many problems. From AD52 to 54 Paul was in Ephesus, on the west coast of Asia Minor, across the Aegean Sea. From there he sent a letter warning the Corinthians against associating with sexually immoral persons. We do not have that letter (although some think part of it can be found in 2 Corinthians 6:14—7:1), but Paul refers to it in 1 Corinthians 5:9–10. The Corinthians responded with a letter which asked Paul a number of questions (1 Corinthians 7:1; he addresses their questions in 1 Corinthians 7:1ff; 8:1ff; 12:1ff; 16:1ff; 16:12). In addition, some brought him an oral report of their divisions (1:11; 11:18). Paul replied in the letter we know as 1 Corinthians, sent probably sometime in early AD54.

That same year, Paul visited Corinth a second time (2 Corinthians 2:1; 12:14, 21; 13:1–2). On this 'painful' visit, someone publicly insulted Paul and challenged his authority. This person may have been the brother who was living in an incestuous relationship with his stepmother (1 Corinthians 5:1–5), but we lack evidence. Although the offender's action hurt the church, he also sinned against Paul (2 Corinthians 2:10). In any case, the Corinthians stood back and did not support Paul in the confrontation; some of them apparently even demanded proof that Christ spoke through him (2 Corinthians 13:3). The situation may have been made worse by the presence of rival preachers who challenged Paul's authority (see below), but we do not know for certain when they arrived in Corinth.

Paul left in great disappointment, and changed his plans. He had originally expected to visit Corinth again before long, but he decided instead to send a strong letter of rebuke, urging the congregation to discipline the offending brother (2 Corinthians 1:23; 2:1–11; 7:8–13). A number of scholars identify this letter with 1 Corinthians, but the details do not fit well enough to satisfy most commentators today. If we assume that it was not our 1 Corinthians, Titus would have brought the 'severe letter' to Corinth in early AD55.

Late in that year, Titus returned to Paul and met him in Macedonia (north of Greece). Titus brought good news that the 'severe letter' had worked (2 Corinthians 2:5–11; 7:6–16), but bad news in two other respects. Some Corinthians were criticizing Paul as being fickle because he changed his travel plans. More serious was the news that visiting Jewish Christian preachers were taking advantage of the congregation's immaturity, undermining Paul's pastoral authority in Corinth and threatening to lead the believers into serious error. The situation was critical, and Paul's relationship with the church hung in the balance. Paul sent 2 Corinthians in late AD55 or early 56.

Paul's opponents

Paul faced criticism both from within the church and from without. Piecing together bits of information from the letter, we can begin to draw a composite picture of the visiting preachers who threatened Paul's relationship with the Corinthians. However, it is difficult to determine exactly who these opponents were, and whether the criticisms Paul addresses came directly from them or from the Corinthians who were influenced by them.

The intruders were Jewish-Christian itinerant preachers (11:22) who, unlike Paul, carried letters of recommendation from other Christians known to the Corinthians (3:1). Apparently they styled themselves as apostles, but it is very doubtful that these preachers were among Jesus' first disciples. Unlike Paul, they accepted financial support from the Corinthians, as Jesus had instructed (2:17; 11:7; see Luke 10:7; 1 Corinthians 9:14). But they went too far, and their motives were suspect (2:17). They acted in a demanding and heavy-handed way, and did not hesitate to throw their weight around. At least some of them were more eloquent in their speech than Paul (11:5f; 10:10). How much they stressed obedience to the Old Testament law is unclear, but they apparently boasted of revelations and ecstatic visions they experienced (12:1–6) and the wonder-working signs they performed (12:11–13). Either they or the Corinthians drew the conclusion that, by contrast, Paul talked big in his letters, but was weak in person (10:10).

The Jerusalem collection

Besides responding to Titus's news about the effect of his severe letter on the church and about the crisis caused by the visiting preachers, Paul also wanted to motivate the Corinthians to fulfil their promise to contribute to a collection he planned to take back with him for the church in Jerusalem (see 2 Corinthians 8–9).

That collection was something of an obsession with Paul for much of his ministry. Perhaps it had its beginning in Galatians 2:10 when the Jerusalem apostles asked him to remember the poor. Jerusalem needed this money for several reasons. Public dole funds strained to support the widows of the many who had retired to the holy city. Annual pilgrimages for festivals meant the extra cost of providing food and housing for those who couldn't afford it. We know from Acts that the early church in Jerusalem experimented with communal life, but we have no assurance that it was a financial success. Famine was no stranger to the area (see Acts 11:27–30), and some Christians suffered economic persecution for their faith.

Paul mentions the collection in 1 Corinthians 16:1–4 and Romans 15:25–28. Most scholars think that his travelling companions listed in Acts 20:4 were delegates of some of the churches that contributed to the gift. The collection was an act of genuine charity to help the poor. But Paul was also seeking to help his converts to demonstrate the unity of the church— to show conservative Jewish Christians in Jerusalem that those who responded to his message worshipped the same Lord and were part of the same body of Christ. At the same time, he wanted the Gentile Christians in the churches he founded to demonstrate their thanksgiving for the inheritance they had received from Israel. This is speculation, but perhaps Paul also was influenced by the traditions in Isaiah and Micah about the

Gentiles bringing gifts to Jerusalem in the last days (Isaiah 2:2–4; 60:6f, 11; Micah 4:13). He hoped that, like his Lord, his life and work might play a role in helping to fulfil God's promises to his people.

The unity of 2 Corinthians

A few scholars think that 2:14—7:4 seems an unnaturally long digression and therefore could not have been part of Paul's original letter. Similarly, many speculate that since 6:14—7:1 abruptly interrupts the flow of 2 Corinthians, it must originally have belonged elsewhere. Finally, an increasing number of commentators hold that chapters 10–13 form part of either the earlier 'severe letter' (referred to in 2:3–4; 7:8–12), or another letter written after 2 Corinthians 1–9.

The main problem with such theories is the absence of any evidence in the Greek manuscripts to support the omission of these passages from the original letter. It is possible to make a good case for their inclusion (see for instance Ford and Young). Furthermore, we do not know how long Paul paused during the process of dictation. After he completed chapters 1–9, he may have heard fresh news about the opponents that prompted him to compose 10–13 before sending the epistle. As Ford and Young argue, the placement of this discussion at the end may well be deliberate. This book seeks to interpret 2 Corinthians based on its final form as we have it; for other views, readers will want to consult the commentaries listed in the bibliography.

Suggestions for further study

Barnett, Paul. *The Second Epistle to the Corinthians*. New International Commentary on the New Testament. GrandRapids/ Cambridge: Eerdmans, 1997. Recent detailed commentary by an Australian Anglican bishop. Expounds the letter as a unity.

Barrett, C.K. *The Second Epistle to the Corinthians*. Black's New Testament Commentaries. London: A. & C. Black, 1973. Twenty-five years on, it remains one of the best commentaries available; thinks chapters 10–13 belong to a later letter.

Belleville, Linda L. *2 Corinthians*. IVP New Testament Commentary. Downers Grove, IL/Leicester: InterVarsity Press, 1996. Very helpful and practical, with a number of modern illustrations from an American perspective; argues for the unity of the letter.

Best, Ernest. *Second Corinthians*. Interpretation. Louisville: John Knox Press, 1987. Shorter critical commentary that takes 6:14—7:1 to be originally separate and takes 10–13 to be a subsequent letter.

Furnish, Victor Paul. *II Corinthians*. The Anchor Bible. New York: Doubleday, 1984. Very thorough; takes 10–13 to belong to a later letter.

Kreitzer, Larry. *2 Corinthians*. New Testament Guides. Sheffield: Sheffield Academic Press, 1996. Concise introduction to critical issues for serious students.

Kruse, Colin. *2 Corinthians*. Tyndale New Testament Commentaries. Grand Rapids/Leicester: Eerdmans/InterVarsity Press, 1987. Concise conservative evangelical commentary; takes 10–13 to be a subsequent letter.

Martin, R.P. *2 Corinthians*. Word Biblical Commentary. Waco, TX: Word, 1986. Thorough and technical, moderate evangelical commentary; understands 10–13 as a subsequent letter.

Thrall, Margaret E. *A Critical and Exegetical Commentary on the Second Epistle to the Corinthians, Volume I.* International Critical Commentary. Edinburgh: T. & T. Clark, 1994. Very thorough critical study of the Greek text; volume 2 is forthcoming.

Watson, Nigel. *The Second Epistle to the Corinthians*, Epworth Commentaries, London: Epworth Press, 1993. Concise moderate critical commentary; takes 6:14—7:1 to be a non-Pauline insertion and 10–13 to be a subsequent letter.

Witherington, Ben III. *Conflict and Community in Corinth.* Grand Rapids: Eerdmans, 1995.

Young, Frances and David Ford. *Meaning and Truth in 2 Corinthians.* Biblical Foundations in Theology. London: SPCK, 1987. Full of insights into the problems of interpreting the letter and its contribution to the Christian faith; argues for the unity of 2 Corinthians.

Day 1

FOR ALL THE SAINTS

---

2 Corinthians 1:1–2

Paul usually starts his letters in a standard way, reflecting the conventions of his day. Personal letters typically began by identifying the sender, then the recipients, followed by a simple greeting. Paul expands on each of these bits, and his additions give us clues as to what was foremost in his mind at the time. Several features stand out in the salutation introducing 2 Corinthians.

Paul often called himself 'an apostle of Christ Jesus'. Putting 'Christ' (the Greek translation of the Hebrew 'Messiah', or 'anointed one') before 'Jesus' reminds us that 'Christ' was originally a title before it became a proper name. The addition of the words 'by the will of God' shows us that people questioned whether Paul was really 'sent with authority' (the basic meaning of 'apostle') by God. From the very beginning of Paul's ministry, some Christians were understandably suspicious as to whether the faith of their former persecutor was genuine. Conservative Jewish Christians challenged his teaching that Gentiles (non-Jews) did not have to become Jews in order to become part of the people of God. In Corinth, his authority as a Christian leader was being questioned. At the outset, Paul states what he will seek to emphasize later in the letter: his authority as a spokesman for Christ came directly from God.

Another feature is the inclusion of Timothy as a co-sender of the letter. The Corinthians knew him (1 Corinthians 4:17; 16:10f; 2 Corinthians 1:19), and Paul's addition of the words 'our (literally "the") brother' reminds them that they all belong to one spiritual family. How much Timothy actually contributed to the contents of this letter is hard to say, just as it is in the case of Sosthenes, who is mentioned at the beginning of I Corinthians (I Corinthians 1:1). Although Paul uses the plural 'we' in most of 2 Corinthians, much of the letter seems to come directly from him. Despite his strong sense of independence, however, Paul was not a loner. His faith knew the value of companionship. His security in Christ enabled him to share leadership and to delegate responsibility without being threatened. He was also wise enough to know that, given the difficult situation in Corinth, he needed to marshal all the support he could get to maintain the confidence of his hearers!

Perhaps most interesting is the addition of the words 'including *all* the saints *throughout* Achaia' (the Roman province comprising southern Greece). From the rest of the letter, it's clear that Paul is primarily addressing the church in Corinth (the capital of Achaia); why does he expand his audience here? No doubt he hoped that more people would contribute to the collection he was bringing with him to Jerusalem (see the Introduction, and 2 Corinthians 8–9); and Paul often wanted his letters read widely. But we shouldn't forget the history of Greece as a collection of fiercely independent city-states. Paul is subtly reminding the Corinthians, who saw themselves sometimes more as individuals or as groups than as a united body, that they belonged to something larger. That was certainly Paul's concern in I Corinthians (I Corinthians 1:2; see also I Corinthians 4:17; 11:16; 14:33; 16:19). Paul hoped that his hearers would recognize that they were a part of a greater body of Christians, a family whose fellowship and standards were to be shared. *All* Christians are 'saints' (literally, 'holy ones'), inasmuch as God considers us as belonging to him and set apart for service in Christ.

The greeting that follows in verse 2 appears in most of Paul's letters, and reminds us of Paul's Jewish and Christian heritage. The usual word at this point in a Greek letter would be *chairein* ('greetings'). Paul modifies this to *charis* ('grace') which means 'undeserved kindness'. Grace is something seen supremely in Jesus' giving of himself for all on the cross, something Paul himself had experienced when he came to faith in Christ, and something every Christian continually needs in order to live a life that pleases God. To this, Paul joins the word *eirene*, the Greek translation of the Hebrew *shalom* ('peace'). The biblical notion of peace is more than the absence of violence and conflict; it includes wholeness, prosperity and blessing in community. For a Christian, peace is not a private matter of withdrawal from the world, but a right relationship with others. Christians have peace with God (Romans 5:1), and they seek, if possible, to be at peace with all (Romans 12:18).

Questions for thought

1. Individuals who claim to be 'sent by God' make people nervous! Does God still 'send' people and, if so, how can others determine that the calling is true?

2. Why is it important for Christian leaders to share leadership? What hinders them from doing so?

3. If you are an Anglican, do you ever think about the fact that you and your church are members of the Anglican Communion? What difference could that make?

4. How do 'grace' and 'peace' feature in your own life?

Day 2

GOD'S CONSOLATION

2 Corinthians 1:3—11

After the salutation, Paul usually offers a thanksgiving for God's work in the lives of his hearers. In our passage he adopts the language of Jewish synagogue worship: he blesses God (see Ephesians 1:3). Paul focuses on the great comfort and encouragement God gives. That consolation in turn enables him and his companions who are consoled to console others who suffer. As in the salutation, Paul is introducing themes that will recur in the letter.

Ten times in five verses Paul uses the noun *paraklesis* and the related verb *parakalo*, difficult words to translate. The NRSV renders them 'consolation' and 'to console', but these words also carry the idea of encouragement and strengthening. This is the same root that appears in the Septuagint (the Greek translation of the Old Testament), translating Isaiah 40:1; 51:3; 61:2 and referring to the comforting promise that God would deliver his people from affliction. John uses the same root in his gospel to describe the Holy Spirit, the *comforter* (14:16, 26; 15:26; 16:7). Many believe John's Gospel to have been written from Ephesus, and it is striking that, writing about his experience of suffering in that same city, Paul here emphasizes the same root.

What Paul is doing in these introductory verses is expressing confidence in God, establishing a common ground with his hearers, gaining their support, and gently encouraging them to recognize that his sufferings are something they are meant to share. He takes for granted that he and the Corinthians suffer for the sake of Christ, and he will return to the theme of his own suffering repeatedly in the letter (4:7–18; 6:3–10; 7:4–7; 11:23–12:10; 13:3–4). The extent to which the Corinthians themselves had already suffered as Christians is less clear.

For the Christian, the comfort and strength God gives isn't intended to be an end in itself; it issues in further comfort as the comforted become comforters (1:4). God's grace in afflictions has a *transforming effect*; it touches lives in need, with the result that they touch others. We want God to transform our circumstances; God is more interested in transforming *us*.

But Paul is making a further point here. Precisely in our weakness and suffering, God's grace and power appear in his consoling work. In the ancient world, strength was respected and weakness despised. Paul saw in his affliction for the gospel a sharing in the sufferings of Christ, and an opportunity for God's grace to abound as it enabled him to do something he could not do in his own strength. The paradox of God's power being present in human weakness is another theme that recurs repeatedly in the letter. Whereas the Corinthians looked for God's power in great displays of eloquence, signs and wonders (as people often do today), Paul wanted them to appreciate the paradox that God's transforming presence was seen most clearly in Christ's afflictions. Paul's own suffering proved his apostleship and manifested the power of God.

Paul's talk about suffering was nothing abstract, as the lists of hardships in chapters 4 and 11 reveal. In verse 8 of chapter 1, he becomes more specific about a recent crisis. The language he uses is surprisingly frank. Exactly what experience Paul refers to is unknown; suggestions include grave illness, imprisonment at Ephesus (cf. 1 Corinthians 15:32) and, more likely, severe opposition from the Jews there (cf. Acts 19:23–41). At some time he had apparently reached the point of facing certain death, leaving him only with his hope for resurrection.

But God had other plans, and Paul saw a divine purpose in the crisis—it drove him to rely not on himself, but on the one who raises the dead (1:9). Although he may sometimes be thought of as a 'super-Christian', dependence upon God did not come naturally to Paul. It was something he learned repeatedly through the 'ups' and especially through the 'downs' of his Christian experience (see Philippians 4:11). Recollection of how God had rescued him in the past fuelled further confidence that God could be trusted to deliver him in the future (1:10). It pays to take time to remember. Recalling God's faithfulness to us in the past enables us to be more faithful here and now.

Paul concludes this section by enlisting the prayers of the Corinthians (1:11). Although some of the Corinthians had begun to doubt his integrity and question his authority, they could hardly refuse to pray for him and his companions. The surest way to change someone's hostile attitude towards another is to get them praying for them! More than that, Paul believed that prayer actually made a difference, and his ultimate goal was for it to result in thanksgiving to God.

Questions for thought

1. When and how have you ever experienced God's consolation? Did that affect the way you relate to others?

2. Do you find it surprising that an apostle felt 'so utterly, unbearably crushed' that he 'despaired of life itself' (v. 9)? What specifically do you think enabled Paul not to give up and renounce his faith?

3. Does prayer really make a difference? How?

Day 3

A MATTER *of* INTEGRITY

---

2 *Corinthians* 1:12–14

In verse 12 Paul launches into one of the main issues addressed in the letter: his loss of credibility among some of the Corinthians. He knows that he's been criticized for saying one thing and doing another, specifically regarding his travel plans (1:15ff) and his change of tone in an earlier 'severe letter' (2:3–4; 7:8–12; probably not a reference to 1 Corinthians— see the Introduction). Furthermore, earlier he had refused financial support from the Corinthians (1 Corinthians 9:15–18); given his concern to arrange a collection now (purportedly for Jerusalem), certain people may have considered Paul's finances to be suspect. As we shall see, Paul is quite careful to avoid giving any impression of impropriety. His response is robust, but also hopeful and positive.

Paul begins by defending his motives, appealing to his clear conscience. His choice of the word 'boast' (1:12) may seem puzzling, but the word essentially means 'confident pride'. He uses it frequently in the Corinthian letters, both negatively (referring to boasting in human accomplishment in contrast to dependence upon God) and positively, as in this case. Some Christians consider 'pride' to be always inappropriate, but not so for Paul.

He is confident in several respects. First, he and his companions have behaved in a straightforward way. Some Greek manuscripts read *hagiotes* (NIV/NRSV: 'holiness' or moral purity), whereas others read *haplotes* (AV: 'simplicity'; NRSV: 'frankness'). Both make sense, but the latter is more likely the original word, since Paul uses it several times in 2 Corinthians. It describes single-minded commitment, the opposite of cunning or trickery.

The second word he uses is *eilikrineia*, a term that refers to being 'unmixed', and hence pure in motive. It refers to utter sincerity. The combination of these two Greek words expresses integrity and complete freedom from dishonesty. Paul doesn't hesitate to defend his motives here, because he knows that to allow further misunderstandings would only undermine his ministry and message.

Rather than relying on worldly wisdom (self-centred calculation), Paul and his companions have depended on the grace of God, especially in relation to the Corinthians. They've done so by refusing to use techniques to manipulate their hearers, and by not compromising the message of the gospel. Because worldly wisdom would reject as foolishness the notion that, through Jesus' death, God was at work bringing us back to himself, Paul has already spoken at length about how God's wisdom can be seen in the cross (1 Corinthians 1:18–2:16). Unfortunately, other things Paul has said have contributed to a problem.

Verse 13 explains where the problem lies. Apparently some have accused him of saying one thing and doing another (1:17). He may be thinking of his very first letter (1 Corinthians 5:9), or the 'severe letter', but foremost in his mind appears to be what he had said about his plans to visit Corinth in 1 Corinthians 16:5–7. In each case, circumstances had changed, and Paul's subsequent words and actions differed from what he had communicated. Did this mean that he originally intended something else? No, what the Corinthians read and understood from him they could trust (1:13). Unfortunately they only knew some of Paul's circumstances, and letters were a poor substitute for a visit in person. He looked forward to a full understanding that would eventually come about as all the facts emerged.

Paul was committed to a full disclosure of truth because he

knew that on judgment day nothing would be hidden. Despite his problems relating to the Corinthians, he remained hopeful that ultimately he and his hearers would have good reason for pride in each other (1:14; the word for 'boast' is related to the word translated 'boast' in 1:12). The 'day of the Lord Jesus' is the final day when Christ returns in glory to judge the world. Then the Corinthians would recognize that through Paul's apostolic authority and guidance the community had been founded and formed. Paul's goal was to present them to Christ on that day as people pure in heart and deed (1 Corinthians 1:8; 2 Corinthians 11:2). By reminding them of their future, Paul hoped to secure a change in their relationship in the present.

Questions for thought

1. What in the Church can Christians be rightly proud of? What about in your church?

2. Do you think Paul was arrogant in his self-defence? What tactics are legitimate in trying to help others understand our perspective?

3. It is possible to be totally sincere, but sincerely wrong. What can Christians do to help ensure that their actions are right, as well as sincere?

Day 4

A QUESTION *of* RELIABILITY

2 Corinthians 1:15—22

Now Paul gets to the root of the problem. In 1:15—16 he explains his original intention, which was confidently to visit Corinth *twice*, once on the way north to Macedonia, and then returning to Corinth before sailing back to Judea. He had hoped that they would assist him in his journey (cf. Romans 15:24), perhaps by helping him find a ship and giving provisions for the trip back to the Holy Land.

But Paul did not do what he had said. Instead of coming in person on the return journey, he sent a letter (1:23–2:4). Was he 'vacillating' when he did this (1:17)? The word means to be fickle in one's choices and occurs only here in the New Testament; it was apparently the Corinthians' own term to interpret his behaviour. Did Paul make his plans simply according to self-centred human standards (literally, 'according to the flesh', in contrast to the guidance of the Holy Spirit) and deliberately say one thing and mean another? His two rhetorical questions in 1:17 are phrased in Greek to demand the answer, 'No'.

Paul doesn't immediately state the reason why he changed his plans. Instead, he tackles the more serious challenge to his ministry underlying the charge of vacillation. Although he had said 'Yes' he was coming, but 'No' he hadn't come, his attitude towards the Corinthians had never been ambiguous or mixed, but confident, ultimately positive and consistently full of goodwill. Paul feels so passionately about this that he uses an oath ('as God is faithful'), as he does elsewhere (Romans 1:9; Galatians 1:20; 2 Corinthians 1:23, etc.). When he spoke to the Corinthians he didn't 'talk out of both sides of his mouth'; his word was reliable (1:18). If it wasn't, that would (a) call into question the Word he proclaimed (1:19–20) and (b) reflect badly on the one who had commissioned him (1:21–22). So Paul is at pains to defend both, and both in turn support *his* trustworthiness.

The language of 'Yes, Yes' and 'No, No' recalls the teaching of Jesus to speak the truth (Matthew 5:37; see also James 5:12). Paul often echoes Christ's teachings, although he rarely says he's doing that (see 1 Corinthians 7:10; 9:14; 11:24f). He makes it clear in 1:19–20 that the one he and his companions preached didn't change his mind, because all of God's promises are kept in Jesus. Christ is God's gift, his 'Yes' to humanity, utterly reliable and completely trustworthy. Paul's Greek in 1:20 is difficult to translate, but the sense is fairly clear: All of

God's promises are affirmed and fulfilled in Christ. This in turn, is why we say the affirmation 'Amen' (from a word meaning 'true', 'reliable') through his name in our worship and praise to God. Jesus' reliability has enabled us to say our 'Yes' to God.

Paul's reliability is also assured by the God who is at work in his and his companions' lives (1:21–22), although what he says applies equally to all Christians. He names four specific aspects of that work. God *establishes* them in Christ. The word has a legal background and means 'to confirm', 'to make secure'. Paul's security lay not in his grasp of God but in God's grasp of him (see 1 Corinthians 1:8). God *anointed* them. Anointing has a long history in the Old Testament as a sign of consecration to high office; Aaron and his sons were anointed as the first priests (Exodus 28:41), and Saul was anointed Israel's first king (1 Samuel 15:1). It could refer here to Paul's being given authority as an apostle, or to being made part of God's royal people who will reign (1 Corinthians 4:8; Romans 5:17). More likely, it refers to the giving of the Spirit to Paul and to everyone who becomes a Christian (see Acts 10:38; 1 Corinthians 12:13).

With the same Spirit Christians are *sealed* (see Ephesians 1:13; 4:30). In the ancient world, seals protected, authenticated, and expressed someone's ownership of the contents. Finally, God gives the Spirit as an *arrabon*, a 'deposit', 'first instalment' or 'down-payment' as a pledge of a future inheritance (2 Corinthians 5:5; Ephesians 1:14). The God who is so concerned to assure his people in all of these ways could be trusted to lead Paul reliably by the same Spirit.

Questions for thought

1. What can people do to help minimize bad communication and to resolve misunderstandings caused by changes in their circumstances?

2. Are there any promises you've made to others that aren't being kept? What steps can you take to fulfil them?

3. What difference should the fact that Jesus is God's 'Yes' to humanity make in the life of the Church?

4. Which aspect of God's work in 1:21–22 seems most important to you? Why?

Day 5

TOUGH LOVE

---

2 Corinthians 1:23—2:4

Having defended his reliability, Paul now explains why he changed his plans. He stayed away and wrote instead, out of love to spare them greater sorrow, and to give them space to do what needed to be done. The occasion for the pain Paul refers to is unclear (see the Introduction). Evidently someone's behaviour in Corinth was deeply divisive and challenging to Paul's authority (2 Corinthians 2:5–11; 7:7–12), but the Corinthians had not responded until Paul took action.

Paul appeals to God as his witness (1:23), again revealing both his desperate concern and his conviction that his whole life was lived before God's gaze. He stayed away to spare the Corinthians further pain. Immediately, Paul senses that his language could be misunderstood as though implying that he had some kind of dictatorial power. So he seeks to overcome the distance with careful clarity in 1:24, reassuring them of his respect. He and his companions are not lords or rulers over the faith of the Corinthians (see Jesus' warning against this in Luke 22:25 and its echo in 1 Peter 5:3), but co-workers for their joy. He knows they can have joy because, despite their problems, his hearers stand firm in their own faith. Notice how Paul uses every opportunity to build up his readers and affirm them.

Like the rest of us, Paul preferred joy to pain any day. He decided not to make another painful visit (2:1). Because we don't have a full account of all of Paul's contacts with the Corinthians, the Greek text here is ambiguous. Since 2 Corinthians 12:14 and 13:1 state that his coming visit will be his *third* trip, apparently Paul's previous painful visit was the first leg of the journey he had originally planned (1:15). As a result of that visit which didn't go well, Paul found himself 'out on a limb' with the congregation. He had no delight in causing others grief; he found it personally painful as well. He found his joy and delight in those among whom he served (2:2f), so he wrote a letter (2:3) instead of coming in person.

As a pastor, Paul had several options. He could simply have done nothing, permitting the error to continue—and watched it divide and destroy what unity the Corinthian church had. He could have confronted the situation in person, taking the reins and forcefully exercising (or attempting to exercise!) control over the congregation—and either split the church or alienate them altogether. Instead, he chose to write a rebuke, urging them to take the necessary action so that his next visit might be full of joy on both sides. Not only would a visit have hurt the Corinthians; it would also have hurt Paul.

Paul's description of his state of mind when he wrote the severe letter shows us more about his humanity (2:4). The word for 'distress' (*thlipsis*) is the same term he used back in 1:4, 8 about his sufferings in Asia; he was a man under pressure. 'Anguish' appears only here in his letters and means 'acute anxiety'. Paul uses a different word to express his anxiety about his congregations later in 11:28. Likewise, reference to his many tears appears only here, although Luke also remembered him as a man who wept in his ministry (Acts 20:19, 31). Paul's choice was neither a cop-out, nor the easy option. His was the attitude of a good parent towards wayward children. As the commentator Victor Furnish says, Paul's was 'an anguish compounded of worry, fear, and hope, but rooted finally and decisively in love'.

Although it stung and wounded the Corinthians, Paul's rebuke was never intended to hurt them but to reveal his love and concern for them. The author of that golden passage in 1 Corinthians 13 did not see love as something sentimental or as something that ignored or excused behaviour that undermined the community of faith. Love is sometimes tough, and always discerning (Philippians 1:9f; Romans 12:9).

Questions for thought

1. 'The apostolic task is the promotion of joy' (M.E. Thrall). In what concrete ways can a church leader demonstrate that he or she isn't 'lording it over' a congregation but working with them for their joy?

2. In what circumstances would it be right for a church to exercise discipline, and how should it do so?

3. Have you ever had to exercise painful discipline? Was it successful or not? Why?

4. Some feel that it isn't wise for Christian leaders to show their emotions. Do you agree? When and how might it be appropriate ?

Day 6

FORGIVING *an* OFFENDER

2 Corinthians 2:5–11

Paul's previous tearful letter of rebuke had worked. The Corinthians had responded by sharply disciplining the offending person (see 7:6–13). Paul was relieved, but his immediate concern was for the brother (the Greek text indicates the person was a male). In the apostle's call for forgiveness and restitution we see the same kind of transforming grace that people experienced in Jesus.

Paul begins by acknowledging that the pain the brother caused affected all of the Corinthians and not only himself (2:5). This reflects Paul's understanding of the church as a body (see I Corinthians 12), and the interdependence of all believers. It also implies, however, that the offending brother had insulted Paul personally or attacked his leadership. A leader with less security in Christ might have been glad to see the back of such a troublemaker, but not the apostle.

'Punishment' in 2:6 does not mean vindictive punishment, but derives from the word normally translated 'rebuke' (see Luke 17:3; 2 Timothy 4:2). Whatever the reproof decided upon by the congregation (possibly expulsion from the community; see I Corinthians 5:1–5), it was enough, and no further rebuke was needed. Paul was satisfied that the decision taken by the majority here was the right course.

But now the offender should be forgiven (2:7). Paul chooses not the usual word 'to forgive' used in the gospels (*aphiemi*), but *charizomai*, related to his favourite word, 'grace' (*charis*). Forgiveness is fundamentally an act of giving freely, when the forgiver gives up the hurt to enable the possibility of a restored relationship. In addition, Paul wanted the brother to be comforted (*parakalo*, the same word for strengthening emphasized in 1:3–7), so that his sorrow might not be overwhelming. Everyone had suffered in this episode; the word for sorrow here is the same as that for 'pain' in 2:1–5. To be disciplined would have meant the pain not only of broken friendships but also losing face, and care would be needed to restore a person fully to life in the church. The leaders in the congregation would want to ensure that the congregation fully welcomed back the repentant brother. So Paul urges the Corinthians to show the reality of their love for the brother (2:8). In this way, he would be drawn back into fellowship (see Matthew 18:15).

The next verse seems to imply that Paul had doubted the Corinthians' character, but the Greek text indicates that he is actually reassuring his readers: his severe letter was effectively a test which they passed with flying colours. There are two words commonly used for testing in the New Testament. One (*dokimazo*) signifies testing with a view to approval, and another (*peirazo*), testing with a view to failure; we might use the analogy of Ford testing Ford cars and Ford testing Vauxhall cars! Paul uses a word derived from the former word here, as the Corinthians proved their obedience to God.

In 2:10 Paul further assures them that he is fully behind the brother's restoration. They shouldn't withhold forgiveness from the offender out of fear that Paul might not approve. The addition 'if I have forgiven anything' is not denying that Paul himself was offended, but is similar to 2:5 in implying that the offence was primarily against the church. 'In the presence of Christ' indicates the apostle's belief that Christ sees everything he does; it emphasizes that Paul's forgiveness is genuine and has the Lord's approval.

Paul never lost sight of the fact that life is a spiritual battle. For the offending brother, exclusion from the church would have meant exclusion from life in Christ and abandonment to the realm of the Adversary (the meaning of 'Satan'; see 1 Corinthians 5:5). Forgiveness and restitution would prevent the church from being outwitted (the word normally means 'defrauded') and robbed of a member (2:11).

We have no quotation of Jesus or appeal to his example by Paul, but it is clear that, like his Master, the apostle didn't selfishly use his power at the expense of others. He could have played it safe and left the troublemaker outside the church; instead he took risks in valuing the individual. It was vital that the Corinthians show the reality of transforming grace in their life as a community. This meant love that redeems, as well as order that protects.

Questions for thought

1. What are the most profound experiences of human forgiveness that you have encountered?

2. Why is it so hard for people to forgive others?

3. Can you think of situations in which people who have offended have been restored to the life of your church? What difference did their inclusion make?

Day 7

An AROMA of CHRIST

---

2 Corinthians 2:12–17

Paul now resumes explaining his actions after he sent the severe letter. He wants to stress how important the Corinthians' response was to him (2:12–13). At the same time, he wants them to understand that his movements and actions aren't based on his own whim, but are subject to God's authority and guidance (2:14–17).

After his painful visit to Corinth on the way to Macedonia, Paul apparently returned to Ephesus, bypassing the Corinthians. At some point between Macedonia and Ephesus he sent them the severe letter. He then journeyed north to Troas to continue his ministry of preaching the gospel. 'A door was opened in the Lord' for Paul in the sense that he had a God-given opportunity for fruitful ministry (as it was in Ephesus; 1 Corinthians 16:9). But Paul couldn't be content to stay there because he was desperate for news. His mind (literally 'spirit') had no rest, because Titus had not come from Corinth with details of their response. So Paul said goodbye to the Christians in Troas, and travelled across the sea again to Macedonia, a step closer to Corinth. He felt compelled to see Titus who would be coming that way.

Verse 14 reads like a radical shift in thought, as Paul begins what has been described as 'a great digression', an extended reflection on his ministry. The train of thought from 2:13 is not picked up again until 7:6! Although some scholars argue that the intervening material did not originally belong here, no manuscripts indicate any break. Linking 2:14 and what precedes are the ideas of the *progress of the gospel*, and of God's *leading* Paul in a path that includes both pain and joy. Although his ministry has included misery in Asia, criticism in Corinth and unfinished work in Troas, he has something to be thankful about.

Twice before, Paul has said in effect that he is not free to choose his own path—his decisions aren't based on earthly wisdom (1:12, 17). Now he states it clearly in a joyful outburst: he is essentially God's willing prisoner, led about in Christ's triumphal procession (2:14; the AV's 'causeth us to triumph' mistranslates the Greek word, which never has that meaning elsewhere).

The metaphor Paul uses here is complex and foreign to our culture. In the ancient world, a conqueror would sometimes lead his captives as spectacles of shame in a victory procession. How much we should draw from this image is unclear. Paul certainly believed that in his travels for the gospel he and his companions were tokens of Christ's victory and servants of the Lord. But Paul's understanding of ministry was not triumphalistic; participation in the 'parade' meant suffering and shame, just as Christ the conqueror of death had suffered.

There is evidence that during some triumphal processions, incense was burnt. Whether Paul draws further on that imagery or changes metaphors to refer to the odour of sacrifice in the Old Testament, his point is that through the preaching of Christ comes the fragrance of knowing God (2:14b–16). How people respond to the aroma of Christ reveals their spiritual state and their future. Paul sees two distinct groups with no middle ground (see 1 Corinthians 1:18; compare Deuteronomy 30:15–20). Ultimately, either people welcome the message of Christ as a fragrance bringing life, or reject it, leading to further separation from God. Although it would be possible to read these verses as though the final outcome was already determined, Paul's use of the present tense here shows that the process was ongoing and still being decided in human choices.

For the preacher this brings an awesome responsibility. Who is sufficient for such a ministry? Certainly not those who peddled God's word with insincere motives (2:17; for their identity see the Introduction). Many travelling speakers in the ancient world made a living from competing with others in teaching about the ultimate things in life. From the very beginning of the Church there have been those who sought to profit financially from preaching. By contrast, Paul refused to accept payment for declaring the gospel (1 Corinthians 9:3–18;

2 Corinthians 11:7–10; 12:14–18); he spoke with sincerity (see 2 Corinthians 1:12), as one sent from God (see 1:1), and responsibly in the sight of God to whom he was accountable (see 2:10).

Paul's question echoes Moses' response that he wasn't sufficient when God called him (Exodus 4:10; somewhat clearer in the Septuagint than in our English text), and the apostle will go on to develop the comparison in chapter 3. Paul wasn't competent in his own ability to preach the gospel faithfully, but as he relied on God's grace, he found the competence to do so (3:5).

Questions for thought

1. Verses 12–13 show us that, for Paul, pastoral concerns sometimes took precedence over evangelism. What should determine their proper balance?

2. Do you ever think of yourself as a 'captive' of Christ? How might that sort of thinking make a difference in your life?

3. Does paying clergy a salary undermine their effectiveness in preaching the gospel? Are there alternatives?

4. What sort of 'aroma' pervades your church?

Day 8

A LIVING LETTER

2 Corinthians 3:1–3

In Paul's day it was customary for newcomers to bring letters from friends recommending them to those they came to visit. Before his conversion Paul himself carried such letters (Acts 9:2; 22:5), and later in his own epistles he wrote on behalf of others such as Phoebe (Romans 16:1; see also 2 Corinthians 8:22–24; Philippians 2:19–24). But because of his strong belief that God had commissioned him, he never felt the need as a Christian to carry them for himself.

Those who were troubling the Corinthians (see the Introduction) apparently brought their own letters of commendation and sought letters from the church to take with them on the next stage of their travels. They, or perhaps the offending brother at Corinth, had been challenging Paul's authority because the apostle had none when he first came to preach there.

Paul recognizes that he has just been defending himself again, as he did in 1:12–14, and that to have to do so sounds as though he needs such a letter. He phrases both of his rhetorical questions in 3:1 to expect the answer 'No' ('We aren't... are we?'). No self-commendation or written résumé was required because the Corinthians themselves (the Greek is emphatic) were his 'letter of reference'.

He goes on to develop the metaphor further. This letter was not written with ink on papyrus or carved in stone, but written in Paul's heart, and there the Corinthians remained. The grammatical tense of the word 'written' implies a writing in the past that stays indelibly etched. This is Paul's way of repeating his ongoing care and concern for his hearers. He didn't practise 'hit and run' evangelism; he invested his life in those to whom he brought the gospel (see 1 Thessalonians 2:8).

His precious letter is accessible rather than confidential. It could be known and read by anyone who met the church (3:2). The Corinthians show in themselves the transforming power of the sender of Paul's 'letter'—that of the closest friend and highest authority one could ask for—Christ himself. Again we find Paul building up his readers by reminding them, despite their problems, of their resemblance to Jesus. Once upon a time they were isolated individuals, caught up in idolatry, thievery, drunkenness, greed and sexual abuse (1 Corinthians 6:9–11). Now, warts and all, Paul sees in them the handiwork of God. They are Christ's representatives to the world.

In the first century, a secretary typically wrote out a letter as it was dictated, and a traveller carried it to its destination. The

Greek text literally says that the 'letter' was 'ministered by us' (3:3), and modern translations divide as to which of these two duties Paul has in mind here. In any case, he and his companions played a vital role of service. Through Paul's ministry the letter that was the Corinthian church came into being. He will go on to pick up the language of ministry again in 3:6.

This letter was written not with ink (a mixture of charcoal, gum and water in his day), but the Spirit of the living God. For Paul, the Spirit is the distinguishing mark of the Christian (see 1:22). His presence in the life of a believer and in the community of faith makes the major difference between life under the old agreement between God and Abraham's descendants, and life in the new covenant effected in Christ. Before the coming of Jesus and the gift of his Spirit, God made his will for his people clear through the law, written on tablets of stone (the Ten Commandments, Exodus 31:18; Deuteronomy 9:10). Now his family in Christ know his presence and discover his will written in their hearts through the Spirit. Paul's language here echoes the promises of Jeremiah and Ezekiel about a new relationship with God to come (Jeremiah 31:33; Ezekiel 11:19; 36:26).

Paul's critics looked for pledges and evidence on paper, but the apostle focused on God's power at work in people. Transformed lives give a far more powerful testimony than words from a human referee!

Questions for thought

1. If someone were writing a letter of commendation for you, what would it say?

2. One person has said that the acid test of a person's ministry is what happens when he or she leaves. What do you think is meant by that? Do you agree?

3. What do you find most surprising in what Paul says in this passage? Why?

Day 9

CONFIDENCE & COMPETENCE

2 Corinthians 3:4–6

Paul knows that what he has just said about the results of his ministry among the Corinthians sounds very confident indeed. Of course, if Paul wants to rekindle confidence among the Corinthians in his ministry, he needs to reassert his own (see also 1:15; 8:22; 10:2)! Quickly he makes clear the source of this kind of assurance.

First, it is a confidence *through Christ*. The turning point in Paul's life was an encounter with Jesus Christ (Acts 9:15–19). After that, Paul saw Jesus as his Lord, through whom God's purposes were worked out. All things were made through Christ (Colossians 1:16). Through Christ God reconciled the world to himself (2 Corinthians 5:18). Through him Paul experienced divine comfort and consolation in suffering (1:5). He is the 'Yes' in whom all of God's promises are fulfilled (1:20), and through Christ all thanks go to the Father (Colossians 3:17). For Paul there was no confidence apart from that mediated through the person of Jesus.

Second, it is a confidence *towards God*. Paul's confidence was directed towards one whom he knew was powerful, faithful, just and true. God is the source of all comfort (1:3), who can be relied upon (1:9), who gives grace (1:12) and is faithful (1:18). He is the one who establishes and commissions (1:21), who gives the Spirit as a guarantee (1:22) and leads Paul in Christ's triumphal procession (2:14). All this Paul has said in just the first two chapters!

People often say, 'If only I had more faith...', as though more assurance might make a decisive difference in our lives. Here we discover one of the keys to Paul's success as an apostle: what mattered most was not great confidence, but confidence in a great God. What steadied his life was not a firm grip on

God, but God's firm grip on him. That is clear from Paul's third point: his confidence is *not based in himself*; it is independent of his own natural competence (3:5). The word translated 'competent' is that same word translated 'sufficient' only a few verses back in chapter two (2:16). Paul's confidence has nothing to do with his own natural resources. Left to his own devices, he is insufficient.

This doesn't mean that Paul considered himself incompetent or thought it was acceptable to act that way! In fact, in 3:5 he makes it clear that he *is* competent in what he does. His sufficiency, however, has its origin in God, who made him competent for his ministry. A title for God in the Septuagint is 'The Sufficient One'; whether or not Paul has this in mind, his confidence is *from God*. False humility denies the power and gifts that God gives us. True humility acknowledges what we can do by God's transforming grace, and gives thanks for it. That way, God gets the credit.

At this point Paul shifts the focus from himself to his ministry. Specifically, God has made Paul competent for a ministry of a *new covenant* (3:6). We saw in yesterday's text that Paul uses language in 3:3 echoing the promise of a new covenant in Jeremiah 31:33; now this becomes explicit. A covenant is an agreement or contract between two parties defining their relationship, and including benefits and responsibilities. Through the death and resurrection of Jesus God established a new covenant that Jeremiah had prophesied (Luke 22:20; 1 Corinthians 11:25). Unlike the covenant established through Moses, which set out God's relationship with his people through the written law, this new covenant is established in human hearts by the Spirit.

The difference is crucial, because 'the letter kills, but the Spirit gives life'. These words are sometimes misinterpreted to undermine the value of the written text of scripture in general and the Old Testament in particular. Paul, however, certainly believed that what he wrote did not kill (!), and that the law was just, holy and good (Romans 7:12). However, when the written law condemns certain behaviour without giving the power to obey the rules, it kills (Romans 7:10–11; 8:2–4). The Spirit is God's means of giving us the sufficiency of resurrection power.

Questions for thought

1. Although we live in a cynical age, many people still have confidence or faith; they simply don't recognize it in action. They put their confidence in money, power, science, technology, or in the wisdom of the street that says, 'There is no God' or even, 'There is nothing to be confident about.' Where does your confidence lie? Where does it come from?

2. What are your areas of competence? Is it possible to give God the credit in those areas without sounding 'pious'? How?

3. Paul says that God has made a new covenant with us. Have you ever thought about making a covenant with God? What sorts of responsibilities and benefits might be included in it?

4. In what ways does the letter still 'kill' today? How does the Spirit give life in your church?

Day 10

A GREATER GLORY

---

2 Corinthians 3:7–11

Paul now develops the contrast between his ministry and that of the covenant given through Moses and alluded to in 3:3 and 3:6. He uses a type of argument from the lesser to the greater, popular with Jewish teachers: 'if A is true... how much more will B be true?' Paul wants to show that since the old Mosaic covenant began with glory, the ministry of the new covenant must surely have all the more glory.

The NRSV uses the word 'glory' eleven times in these five verses, and in order to make sense of it we need to understand its background. In the Old Testament, the Hebrew *kavod* originally meant 'heavy', 'weighty', or 'substantial', and hence, something of worth. People who had glory manifested that glory in their appearance and created an impression on others: God's glory was seen in his splendour or radiance.

The Greek word chosen to translate *kavod* in the Septuagint had a different origin and meaning. *Doxa* referred to someone's 'opinion' or 'reputation'. Now if we remember that Paul's reputation was at stake in Corinth, we can begin to see why 'glory' will become a crucial word in this letter. In Greek and Roman culture, people were expected to seek 'glory' as a high reputation, with its accompanying pride and status. Paul, however, rejects that kind of 'glory' and normally uses 'glory' in the biblical sense. He does not seek 'glory' from people, but that does not mean that his ministry is without glory. In fact, even more of God's splendour can be seen in the covenant Paul preaches than in that of Moses.

The covenant chiselled in stone certainly came in glory. Paul refers here to the giving of the Ten Commandments, when the skin of Moses' face shone after he talked with God (Exodus 34:29–32). But the glory of the new covenant is greater for three reasons. First, there is life because of the Spirit (3:7–8). In Old Testament times people had little if any hope for life beyond the grave. The Holy Spirit normally came upon certain individuals (such as Gideon and Saul) only occasionally and temporarily to enable special acts of power. With the new covenant, the Spirit has come to indwell every Christian, guaranteeing God's acceptance of us (1:22), writing his will in our hearts (3:3) and giving us life (3:6). The future tense in 3:8 'will come' (literally 'will be') points to the Spirit's role in our resurrection and transformation at Christ's return, when God's splendour will be revealed in us (Romans 8:18, 23; 1 Corinthians 15:43).

Second, Paul's ministry has a greater glory because it brings *justification* instead of *condemnation* (3:9). Although it is a gift from God, providing a way for his people to relate to him, the law pronounces a curse on those who fail to keep it (Deuteronomy 27:26; Galatians 3:10). People inevitably fail, and the result is separation from God; in this sense Moses' ministry brought death (3:7). By contrast, Paul brought a message of justification ('acquittal' or 'righteousness'), declaring that God has put us back into a right relationship with himself because of what Jesus has done for us on the cross. If a ministry of death came with splendour, a ministry leading to resurrection life overflows with glory!

Third, whereas the old covenant and its glory were temporary, the new is permanent (3:10–11). Although Moses' skin shone after God gave him the commandments, Paul says the splendour faded (3:7). It was temporary (although the Old Testament is silent about this), and no splendour at all compared to the glory of what has come, just as the light of the moon is nothing compared to the rising sun. Similarly, the old covenant itself was temporary (Galatians 3) until the coming of the Jesus who fulfilled it. He is the fulness of glory (compare John 1:14), and his covenant remains.

Paul's contrast between the covenants doesn't mean that he had come to despise his Jewish heritage or thought little of it (although knowing Christ certainly meant more to him than anything in his past; see Romans 3:1–2; 9:4–5; Philippians 3:7–8). The fact that he contrasts the ministries in particular probably indicates that some of the opposition he experienced in Corinth came either from non-Christian Jews or from the visiting preachers who emphasized the law of Moses.

Questions for thought

1. What does the word 'glory' mean to you? In what sense(s) is there 'glory' in Christian ministry?

2. Which of the three reasons Paul cites do you find most important?

3. It's often said that 'the good' can be the enemy of 'the best'. How do you think non-Christian Jews would respond to the sort of points Paul is making here? Is this anti-Semitic? How would Paul have responded?

Day 11

A TRANSFORMING VISION

2 Corinthians 3:12–18

This passage is one of the most evocative yet difficult sections of the letter to interpret. To understand the main point it is best to read verses 12–13 and 18 together, and to recognize that what Paul writes is basically a commentary on Exodus 34:33–35. Those verses tell how, after Moses finished giving God's commandments to the Israelites, he would cover his face with a veil until the next time he met with the Lord. Exodus doesn't say exactly why, although it could be interpreted to imply that Moses did so because the people were afraid of the shining (Exodus 34:30). According to Paul, however, the purpose of this veiling was to prevent the people from seeing that God's glory reflected in Moses' face was fading away. In contrast, confident that the glory of the new covenant is leading to transformation into ever greater glory, Paul acts with great boldness (*parresia*).

Parresia—courage to speak the truth boldly, frankly and openly—and the verb derived from it are favourite words of Luke to describe the effect of the Spirit in the early Christians in Acts (for example, 2:29; 4:13, 29, 31; 14:3; 19:8; 28:31). Likewise, Paul links his freedom to speak openly with the Spirit who makes the crucial difference (3:17). This is all part of his answer to the charges of being deceitful and inconsistent (1:13, 17—2:4). In contrast, by veiling himself, Moses was not totally frank and open with God's people. Paul will vigorously reassert his own boldness again in chapter 10.

A problem that Paul wrestles with at length in Romans 9–11, and apparently an issue for him in Corinth, is the fact that many Jews were not responding to his message of the new covenant. According to Paul, the Israelites and his Jewish contemporaries have not understood the significance of the veil and Moses' fading glory. Their minds have been hardened (see Psalm 95:8; Romans 11:7, 25) so that they don't see that the old covenant is temporary, finding its goal in Christ (Romans 10:4). Paul spent much of his Christian life preaching Jesus to his fellow Jews (see 1 Corinthians 9:19–20), who in turn refused the new covenant and who continued to depend on the law as if it were permanent. Their response showed Paul that a veil lay over their heart, concealing Christ from them. But when a person does turn to the Lord by faith in Jesus, the veil is removed (3:16), just as Moses lifted his veil when he went to meet with God (Exodus 34:34).

Paul knows that the miracle of accepting Jesus as God's yes to his promises is something only the Spirit can accomplish (see 1 Corinthians 2:12–14). His declaration that 'the Lord is the Spirit' continues to puzzles commentators. The simplest explanation is that, through the Spirit, in the new covenant one experiences the presence of the same Lord that Moses met. The Spirit gives freedom from condemnation and death, and courage to share the message of Christ with boldness.

This leads Paul to another outburst rich with imagery (3:18). With the words 'all of us' Paul includes every follower of Jesus. Moses' encounter with God in private has now become an experience for all believers in their relationships with each other. Christians have 'unveiled faces' inasmuch as the glory is no longer hidden from each other, and we can minister without embarrassment from fading splendour. The following Greek text could mean either 'beholding' or 'reflecting' 'the glory of God as in a mirror', but both ideas appear to be present. We see God's glory just as Moses did, but now we see it reflected in the lives of one another. His splendour shines in the person in the next pew.

To be a Christian is to change, for God is in the transformation business (Romans 12:2). He transforms us progressively into Christ's image (4:4), *as we see* the glory as though reflected in a mirror. This is not an instantaneous change, but a lifelong process of transformation from one state to another. Paul links it directly to the vision of glory in one another. That assumes a transforming community; Paul has no conception of a 'lone ranger' style of Christianity for individuals who remain aloof from the fellowship of the church.

Our transformation leads ultimately to a glorious resurrection body like that of Jesus (Philippians 3:20–21; Romans 8:11). This is the work of grace through the Spirit. Through our successes, failures and sufferings, he works within us both individually and as Christian communities, to conform us to the image of the Son.

Questions for thought

1. How does Christian boldness show itself today in your church? In your life?

2. In what ways have you changed as a Christian in the last five years?

3. Exactly what do you think Paul is thinking about when he speaks of our being transformed from one degree of glory to another? How is that 'glorious'?

4. How has Moses' encounter with God 'now become an experience for all believers in their relationships with each other'?

Day 12

A MINISTRY *of* GLORY

2 Corinthians 4:1–6

There were plenty of reasons why Paul could have lost heart and become lazy or burned out in his ministry. He faced a constant temptation to compromise his message and methods in order to please people and ease the challenge of the gospel. At times he saw little fruit from his preaching, and as we have already seen, he felt the burden of Jewish unbelief. Nevertheless, what urged him on was the mercy of God (4:1). He never forgot

God's kindness that transformed him from a persecutor into an apostle (I Corinthians 15:9–10; Galatians 1:13–16).

Paul refused to engage in behaviour that would cause disgrace if discovered—a good test for temptations we experience today (4:2). He spells out what he means in the words that follow. He didn't believe that the end justifies the means (the word translated 'practise cunning' by the NRSV literally means 'doing everything'); hence he refused to distort God's word. To make life more comfortable for himself and his hearers he could easily water down at least three elements of his message: (1) the cross (crucifixion being a most shameful death in the ancient world); (2) freedom for Christians from having to keep the Jewish laws (to keep Jews and conservative Jewish Christians happy); and (3) the uniqueness and lordship of Christ. The first of these has already surfaced as a Corinthian issue in 1 Corinthians 1:18–2:2; the second and third appear in our passage today.

Instead of diluting the gospel in order to gain superficial success, Paul openly stated the truth in his preaching. Clearly, he believed that people have the capacity to recognize honesty and truth when they see it. Simply by faithfully doing what God called them to do, he and his companions in effect revealed themselves to be obedient. He knows that the message is inseparable from the messenger; unfortunately, sometimes the life of the latter gets in the way of the former. Paul has already refused to commend himself in 3:1, and he will not do it here—his ministry does it for him. The key words 'in the sight of God', reiterate Paul's accountability to his master.

Although the gospel is true, not all receive it (4:3). Apparently Paul is responding to criticism from those who felt that his message of the cross was obscure. The word 'veiled' is related to the same Greek word used in 3:13–16, so Paul may be thinking of Corinthian Jews who have rejected the gospel. In any case, Paul concedes that his message is veiled to some, but that is no fault of his own—the problem lies in the minds of those who are perishing (see 2:15).

Paul never denies that people are responsible for their choices, but behind human rejection of the message he sees the work of a spiritual adversary. 'The god of this age' most likely refers to Satan. Unlike the true God who opens closed hearts (Acts 16:14) and shines his light into them (4:6), Satan blinds the minds of those who do not believe (2:11; 11:14; see 2 Thessalonians 2:9–10). As a result unbelievers' eyes are veiled, so that they cannot see the light (the truth) of the good news about Christ's glory. Christ's 'glory' means his demonstration of God's character and power, seen particularly in Jesus' crucifixion and resurrection.

A focus on Christ's glory, rather than his own, distinguished Paul from other travelling speakers in his day who promoted themselves (4:5). Although some might accuse Paul of talking about himself when he told his 'story', he preached another person—Jesus Christ as *kyrios*, Lord. The notion that Christ is Lord invited criticism both from Jews, who insisted that God alone is Lord, and from Gentiles, whose pluralistic and polytheistic culture taught that there are many lords. Nevertheless, Jesus as Lord formed the centre of authentic Christian proclamation (Acts 2:36; 16:31; Romans 10:9). With this understanding, Christians see themselves primarily as slaves (*douloi*; the word is stronger than *diakonoi*, 'servants') of others, because of what Jesus their Lord has done.

Verse 6 explains the reason why Paul preaches Christ as Lord: the glory of God is seen in Jesus, a reality which God revealed to Paul when he first came to faith. The god of this world may blind people, but the God of creation, who brought light into what was darkness, has shone his light in Paul's heart, making him a new creation (5:17). He did this to show Paul his glory in the face of Jesus, which Paul saw on the Damascus road. Those today who wish to see God's splendour can do no better than to look at Jesus, the very image of God.

Questions for thought

1. In what ways are contemporary preachers tempted to compromise the gospel message? What steps could be taken to encourage faithful preaching of Jesus as Lord?

2. Does belief in a supernatural adversary necessarily lead to avoidance of responsibility?

3. What 'gods' of this world blind people to faith in Christ today?

Day 13

TREASURE *in* CLAY POTS

---

2 *Corinthians* 4:7–12

Paul has spoken at length about the glory of his ministry and the glory of Christ. But he doesn't want the Corinthians to get the wrong idea. This glory isn't a triumphalistic display of splendour, but paradoxically a glory seen in his suffering. Through Paul's *afflictions* God's great power appears, just as it did in the sufferings of the Christ Paul preaches.

Virtually every home in Paul's day had clay pottery for daily use. The material was plentiful and cheap, but fragile and easily cracked or broken. Paul likens himself and his companions to earthenware or clay vessels. They are weak and nothing to boast about, but they hold a treasure far more lasting and valuable— the transforming gospel of Jesus Christ. Paul sees a purpose in this stark contrast between a powerful message and its weak container: it makes it clear that the extraordinary power in their ministry is God's, not theirs. Once again Paul delights in giving God the full credit, unlike those who seek an inflated glory of their own.

In verses 8–9, he illustrates what he means by 'clay jars' with a series of four examples of how God's transforming grace continues to maintain them through desperate straits. Although afflicted (literally 'hard-pressed'; see 1:6) in every way, they aren't completely overwhelmed. They are perplexed (a state of serious anxiety), but do not remain utterly at a loss— although Paul could feel this way at times, since he's already used the latter word to describe his experience in Asia (1:8). Frequently persecuted for their faith, they aren't deserted by God (see Hebrews 13:5). Although knocked down (the Greek can mean hurt severely), they don't perish (the same word used of unbelievers in 2:15 and 4:3). In each case Paul uses the present tense, because these experiences *characterize* his ministry, and he knows his suffering isn't over. A more specific list of his trials will come in 11:23–33.

Paul sums up and concentrates the kind of trials mentioned in 4:8–9 in the imagery of carrying around in his body the death of Jesus (4:10). The word for death here refers to the ongoing process and is better translated 'dying'. As he travels about in his ministry, he exhibits in himself the dying of Jesus. Instead of emphasizing his own power as a worker of signs and wonders like Jesus, Paul prefers others to see his resemblance to his lord in suffering as Jesus suffered.

But Paul isn't talking simply about a *resemblance*. Following Jesus must include taking up his cross (Luke 9:23), because to know Christ is to *share* in his sufferings and to be conformed to his death (Philippians 3:10f). For Paul, suffering is fundamental to being 'transformed from glory to glory into the image of Christ' (see also Romans 8:17). Elsewhere he teaches that Christians are joined and deeply identified with Christ; they have died with him, so that as he was raised from the dead they too might walk in newness of life (Romans 6:3–4). What sustains Paul as he exhibits the dying of Christ, and what enables him to press on is that resurrection life of Jesus. The Greek makes it clear that the *purpose* of carrying his death is so that at the same time, the life that he imparts may be manifested or clearly seen.

Verse 11 restates and strengthens the point made in 4:10. Paul and his companions are constantly being given over (the same word used of Christ's being handed over to the authorities to be crucified) to death in their ministries because of Jesus. But God is at work to demonstrate the living power of his Son. Paul changes the word 'body' (*soma*) to mortal 'flesh' (*sarx*), in order to emphasize that it is through our weak and fragile human existence that God works his wonder of transformation.

The Corinthians were tempted to judge their leader's power and authority by his strength, displays of power, and control. Paradoxically, their salvation depended on human weakness and suffering, seen first in Jesus and then replicated in the life of his followers. The result of that suffering was life. The commentator Linda Belleville observes that, like the Corinthians, people today want to control their circumstances and to operate from a position of strength. Paul's description of his ministry sounds just the opposite. It's precisely when we no longer control the situation that we are in a position to experience God's transforming grace.

Questions for thought

1. What use is there for 'cracked pots'? What weaknesses and limitations in your life make room for God to reveal himself?

2. What does this passage say about the nature of power, and how it should be used?

3. In what way is the dying of Jesus manifested in your church and in your life?

Day 14

A FAITH LEADING *to* GLORY

2 Corinthians 4:13–18

Paul is willing to suffer for Christ and thus to carry about in his body the dying of his Lord because he believes that despite his present hardships, the future is ultimately bright. Four factors enable and feed this persevering faith: the work of the Spirit (4:13), Paul's knowledge of his future hope (4:14, 17), his concern for the Corinthians (4:15a), and his desire to bring glory to God (4:15b). Like his awareness of the mercy of God, they combine to prevent him from growing slack in his ministry or losing heart (4:16; see 4:1).

The 'spirit of faith' (4:13) could refer simply to Paul's spiritual state or disposition. Given the references to the Spirit in chapter 3 and Paul's use of the phrase 'the same Spirit' in I Corinthians 12:8, 9, 11, however, it more likely refers to faith as sustained by the life-giving Holy Spirit (editors of English translations must decide whether to capitalize 'Spirit' or not because the Greek manuscripts made no distinction). Paul's is the same kind of faith found in the Old Testament, which was inspired by the same Spirit who gives the apostle the boldness to preach.

Paul quotes Psalm 116:10 where, in the midst of affliction, the psalmist speaks out because he relies on God. Spirit-driven faith moves people to speak (Romans 8:15–16). Sometimes that speech takes the form of complaint to God (as in the case of the psalmist), but at least communication is taking place, and God wants us to bring our troubles to him. Faith leads Paul to do the same (12:8), although here 'we speak' probably refers to declaring the gospel (see 2:17).

A second factor that strengthens Paul's faith is his knowledge. He doesn't need a PhD to know that the one who raised Jesus from the dead has a plan for those who share in Christ's suffering. The future includes resurrection and being gathered *together* with the Corinthians to be in God's presence (see I Thessalonians 4:13–17). Knowledge of our secure future in Christ can make us take risks in the present which we would otherwise never dare.

Third, all the hardships Paul suffers are for the Corinthians' sake. Some may caricature him as a man carried away with doctrine, but Paul cares about people. Throughout his letters we see that when they suffer, he suffers; when they rejoice, he rejoices (Romans 12:15). He perseveres because he wants to see God's grace transforming their lives into something better. He longs for the ripples of grace to spread further from one life to another, producing an ever-growing chorus of thanksgiving to God.

Thanking God is so important because it's an act of faith (sometimes very costly) that glorifies him—our fundamental responsibility to our creator (Romans 1:21). The fourth and ultimate factor that drives Paul is a passion for giving God glory. That goal gives direction to his behaviour (I Corinthians 10:31).

As a result, Paul presses on. Writing in his fifties, he knows that physically he's gradually wearing out, and he uses strong language to express that (the Greek word normally means 'to be utterly destroyed'). But as he faces suffering in his ministry and the inevitable advance of outer decay, he sees a daily, progressive renewal taking place inside (see Ephesians 3:16). The two processes are related. As he responds by faith through the grace of God to his hardships, he is being transformed from one degree of glory to another (3:18). This renewal is rooted in the knowledge that all of his afflictions, though real and painful, are only slight and momentary in comparison to the lasting, substantial and incalculable splendour that awaits him on the other side (see Romans 8:18). Those afflictions are actually 'producing' that weight of glory. Paul suffers with Christ in order to be glorified with him (Romans 8:17).

Paul's assurance of his future affects his focus in the present (4:18). Our English word 'scope' comes from the same Greek root as the word here translated 'look at'. It means 'to watch closely', 'to continue to take careful notice'. His heart is set not on that which is temporary, but on what lasts. The context (and particular the verses that follow) indicates that Paul is thinking about his body which is wearing away, in contrast to the resurrection body he will one day have. The contrast is thus not between what is currently visible and invisible, but between what is now and what will be when Christ is revealed (Romans 8:23–25; I Corinthians 15:50–53).

Questions for thought

1. What factors keep you going in your Christian life?

2. Do you agree that the expression of anger or complaint to God is a sign of faith? Why or why not?

3. What can the church do to increase thanksgiving, to the glory of God?

4. Given Paul's concern to look at things which are lasting, do you think he would have watched television, if it were available in his day? If so, what would he watch?

Day 15

A MATTER *of* LIFE & DEATH

---

2 Corinthians 5:1–10

The division of text at the start of chapter 5 breaks into the middle of Paul's reflection about the contrast between his present body which is wasting away and his future life in glory. Our passage today tells us more about his expectation for life after death, when the 'earthly tent' of his body is gone. It shows us his confidence and longing for a future home that is eternal. As he speaks, Paul assumes quite a bit of understanding on the part of his Corinthian hearers, so to grasp Paul's thought we need some background.

The Greeks believed that the body is a prison for the soul, and that after death people exist solely as spirit (if at all), without a body. For the Jews, however, the body is inseparable from human existence and defines who we are; they generally could not conceive of life without one. That's why it's hard to find much hope in most of the Old Testament for people who had died. Blessing was only possible if our bodies were alive to enjoy it! Only when a notion of resurrection developed could Jews began to speak of 'eternal life' in an 'age to come' (see Dan 12:2). Paul didn't depart from his Jewish heritage in this respect. His teaching here builds on a foundation already laid for the Corinthians in I Corinthians 15:35–57, which should be read alongside our passage.

Interpreters debate the meaning of the 'building from God' in 5:1. It could refer to heaven, the Father's house (John 14:2), or to the 'temple' of Jesus' resurrection body (Mark 14:58). The parallel with the 'earthly tent' however supports a reference to Paul's own resurrection body. Paul's 'groaning' in 5:2, 4 is for the same cause as his groaning in Romans 8:23 (the only other place he uses the word), where he longs for the 'redemption' of his body. The change will take place when Christ transforms our lowly bodies to be like his own glorious body at his return (Philippians 3:20–21; I Corinthians 15:51–54).

But what about all those in the faith who die before Christ returns? What is their state now? These questions have led some to understand our passage to refer to an 'intermediate state' between death and resurrection life. When people 'take off' 'this tent' (shed their earthly body in death), are they 'naked' and 'unclothed' (having no body until the final resurrection), although their spirit is with the Lord (5:8)?

It is more likely, however, that the 'nakedness' in 5:3 refers not to a Christian state of existence in between death and resurrection, but to the view Paul argued against in I Corinthians 15, namely that people will have no body after death. Paul isn't really addressing questions about an 'intermediate state' here, much as we might wish him to. The more he suffers, the more he groans while he has a body subject to suffering and decay, not because he wants to be without a body (as though the body were something bad), but because he longs for a further clothing—a glorious resurrection body that supersedes and is a transformed version of his present weak one (5:4).

Paul can have courage (a better translation than the NRSV's 'confidence') in his trials because God is at work in his life now (5:5–6, 8). He is preparing Paul for this final transformation. He guarantees Paul's future through the gift of his Spirit as a 'first instalment' (see 1:22) towards that end.

Paul knows joy in life, but he doesn't dread death. He prefers to be absent from his earthly body and at home with the Lord (5:8), and sees death as a doorway to something much better than earthly life (Philippians 1:21, 23). But he doesn't seek escape from his body, because his life has a purpose. Paul aims to please God, aware that ultimately he is accountable for what he does with what he has been given. In the ruins at Corinth today there remains an impressive stone, the *bema* or judgment seat where Paul may have been brought before Gallio to be judged (Acts 18:12–27). Paul reminds the Corinthians that one day we must all appear before the *bema* of Christ (see Romans 14:11–12; Matthew 25:31–46). Paul looks to that day with courage, because of his trust in a good God who is at work in him to enable his purposes.

Questions for thought

1. What are the implications of the Jewish/Christian perspective about the body for how we treat our bodies and for what we do with them?

2. Would this understanding of the body have anything to say about the way we relate to others who suffer?

3. List the things we can learn from this passage about life after death. Which of these do you think is most important?

4. Someone has said that a person is not really ready to live until he or she is ready to die. Do you ever think about your own death? What effect does that have on you?

Day 16

MOTIVES *for* MINISTRY

2 Corinthians 5:11–15

Part of the motivation for Paul's ministry was the prospect of final judgment (5:10) and his 'fear' of God. The AV's 'terror' is too strong a translation for this word, but 'reverence' is too weak. A healthy 'fear' of our awesome Creator and Redeemer— as Lucy feared Aslan in C.S. Lewis's *The Chronicles of Narnia*— should keep us from thinking we can ever control him or confine him to our own ideas. The first Christians held together the comfort of the Spirit and fear of the Lord (Acts 9:31), the 'beginning of wisdom' (Proverbs 1:7; see Deuteronomy 10:12; Proverbs 16:6).

That concern led Paul to do his best to *persuade* others of the truth of the gospel. He knew he had a role to play in God's work of transforming people's minds, hearts and lives. He persuaded them, not with deceptive techniques or hollow eloquence, but with the straightforward message of God's love seen in the cross and resurrection of Christ, and the reality of divine judgment (1 Corinthians 15:3–4; Acts 17:31). We can all thank God that Paul didn't view Christianity as a private concern only to be kept to himself; otherwise, the Church might not exist today. He believed that the message of the gospel was *public* truth, and we lose that perspective at our peril.

What was also public and manifest was his life. The Greek verb that is translated 'are well known' twice in 5:11 is the same word rendered 'appear' in the previous verse about the future judgment. Just as his life will one day be laid bare when he stands before Christ at the heavenly judgment seat, it is already plain in the sight of God, who knows very well Paul's inner motives and what he is about. Likewise, Paul hopes his integrity will be clear to the consciences of the Corinthians.

But this sounds like boasting or commending himself again, so once more Paul anticipates a misunderstanding (5:12; see 3:1; 4:2). He's trying to give the majority of Christians in Corinth a reason to be proud of him in response to those who criticize him for lacking machismo, eloquence and wonder-working power (5:12; 10:10; 11:5; 12:1, 11). What matters most is a heart that is submitted to God and is true. Here and in the following verse, Paul is motivated by concern for the Corinthians.

Verse 13 apparently reflects criticism of Paul. We get our English word 'ecstasy' from the root translated 'to be beside ourselves'. Here it could refer either to being crazy (NIV: 'out of our mind') or to experiences of being caught up in religious ecstasy. Some people thought Paul's faith was crazy (Acts 26:24; as Jesus' family once thought him mad—Mark 3:21). Others criticized him for not outwardly showing more religious fervour. In Corinth, ecstatic experiences were seen as signs of spirituality, and highly prized (1 Corinthians 12–14).

Whether Paul is thought to be crazy or not ecstatic enough, that is for God to judge; Paul isn't out to impress others. Either way, his behaviour isn't driven by self-interest, but by sober-minded concern for the benefit of the Corinthians.

What does drive and press Paul onward is an overwhelming sense of the 'love of Christ' (5:14). The phrase could mean Paul's love for Christ or vice versa. The following words favour the latter, because Christ's death on our behalf supremely demonstrates his love (Romans 5:8; Galatians 2:20; Ephesians 5:2). Fear may sometimes lead people to do the right thing, but there is no motivating power greater than that of knowing we are loved, especially when that love is costly.

Jesus died 'for all'. The little word translated 'for' can mean simply 'on behalf of', or more specifically, 'in the place of' (understanding Christ's death as a substitution). Certainly he achieved something for us on the cross that we could never do for ourselves. But if he died in our place, how does it follow that 'therefore all have died', and in what sense have they died? The answer appears in the following verse (5:15). Those united to him by faith (5:17) cannot go on living for themselves because Christ's death means for Christians a death to self-interest (see Romans 6:2–4, 11; Galatians 2:20).

Questions for thought

1. How does 'fear of the Lord' relate to our belief that God loves us? Can fear be a legitimate motivation for sharing the gospel today? What role, if any, does the 'fear of the Lord' play in your life?

2. Many view religion as a private matter of no concern to the next person, and feel that it is wrong to try and change others' opinions. Do you agree?

3. What examples of sacrificial love have you seen in the life of others?

Day 17

A MINISTRY
of RECONCILIATION

---

2 Corinthians 5:16—21

This passage follows on closely from the preceding verses, as Paul explains the consequences of the death and resurrection of Jesus for believers, for the world, and for Paul's ministry— particularly for his work with the Corinthians.

Being a Christian leads to a different way of looking at people (5:16). No longer does Paul regard others from simply a human/worldly point of view (literally 'according to the flesh'). This means not evaluating people according to their outward circumstances, in the way that some have evaluated his ministry. Once upon a time, as a non-Christian Pharisee, he thought Jesus couldn't possibly be from God since he was clearly under the curse of the Old Testament law, having been hung on a tree (Galatians 3:13). Then, on the road to Damascus, Paul came to realize that Jesus was actually the Messiah who suffered on the cross on his behalf.

Paul restates his point in 5:17. To be 'in Christ' (a way of referring to being a Christian, emphasizing 'belonging') is to be a new creation: the old life has ceased to exist (see 5:14: all died) and new things have come into being. It means becoming a part of a process of the re-creation of God's world which will one day culminate in resurrection, and a new heaven and earth (Romans 8:19—23). Although some English translations may imply it, Paul isn't saying that *everything* is new for a Christian. Our personality and circumstances don't normally change overnight! Nevertheless, when people recognize that Jesus has died to restore their broken relationship with God, and when they claim that for themselves by faith, they pass from death to life. By God's grace a transformation has begun, bringing a completely new outlook.

The death and resurrection of Jesus, and every part of the resulting new creation, including Paul's ministry, has come from God (5:18). Like Peter and the first Christians, Paul considers the cross to be no accident, but part of a divine plan to bring people back into relationship with God (see Acts 2:23; 4:27–28). The apostle doesn't say that God needed reconciling to us; it is we who moved away from God, so that a divine initiative of grace in Jesus was needed to bring us back.

Verse 19 expands on 5:18 and gives us in a nutshell the good news Paul preached. Through the person of Christ, God was reconciling the world (Jews and Gentiles) to himself. Although trespasses (failure to do his will or keep his law) created a barrier between humanity and its creator, God didn't take that into account: human failures didn't prevent him from demonstrating his love by dealing with the obstacle of sin (5:21). The context makes clear that the *means* of reconciliation referred to isn't through the teachings or example of Jesus, life-giving as they are, but through Christ's death, the centre of Paul's message (see 1 Corinthians 1:23; 2:2).

In Christ, God acted to reconcile the world to himself, but that reunion can only take place in people's lives if they receive it for themselves (5:20). To that end God has given Paul a ministry of preaching his reconciling grace in Jesus. Paul and his co-workers are ambassadors, representing God who appeals (the same Greek word used of the comforting, consoling work in 1:4, 6) through them to humanity. They appeal *on Christ's behalf*, a point emphasized by its repetition and seen through the sufferings they share with him. They declare what has been done, and call for people to receive reconciliation and a new relationship with God by coming back through faith in Jesus. Although people may sometimes feel that God has abandoned his world, we are the wanderers, and he the seeker.

We hear in 5:20 the voice of Paul's evangelistic ministry, as he speaks directly to the Corinthians. He 'entreats' them, using a verb normally used in prayers or when earnestly begging another, to be reconciled to God. Obviously, he isn't calling them to an initial faith, since his hearers are already Christians. But inasmuch as they are questioning his apostolic authority (and thus his message), they need to return to a right spiritual orientation. He will go on to entreat them again in 6:1–3, 13; 7:2–4.

In 5:21 Paul seeks to motivate the Corinthians to respond to his call. He gives us a glimpse into what was really taking place in the death of Christ. The sinless one became 'sin' (probably to be understood in terms of an Old Testament sin-offering; Romans 8:3; compare Hebrews 10:5–10) on our behalf, so that in Christ we might become 'righteous' (in right relationship with God, and sharing Jesus' character). In some profound way, an exchange took place. Jesus became as we are, so that we might become as he is, a wondrous idea that reappears in a different form in 8:9.

Questions for thought

1. Do you think of yourself as a new creation? What has changed?

2. What does Paul's understanding of his ministry in these verses have to say about the way we communicate the gospel today?

3. What implications does reconciliation with God have for relationships with others?

Day 18

MARKS *of* AUTHENTIC MINISTRY

2 Corinthians 6:1–13

Paul is finally rounding up the defence of his ministry and returning to the Corinthians' situation. He has just reminded them that he is an ambassador for Christ through whom God is appealing to them (5:20). Now reiterating that he works together with God, Paul appeals directly once more (6:1). If they reject Paul's authority, they are rejecting the one who sent him. A refusal to be reconciled to God's ambassador and thus to God raises a big question mark over their spiritual state. This evokes a warning and an invitation (6:1–2). Paul reminds them of the marks that show his ministry to be authentic (6:3–10). He has been open to them; now they should be open to him (6:11–13).

We shouldn't underestimate Paul's anxiety and the seriousness of his warning not to receive God's grace in vain (6:1). To know the truth and then to turn away from it is worse than never to have known it at all; God's undeserved kindness is spurned and comes to no effect. This is a decisive moment for the Corinthians. Paul quotes from Isaiah 49:8, where the Lord declares to Israel that, having listened to their troubles, he will act to deliver them. Paul sees God's deliverance *par excellence* having taken place in this age through Jesus, and *now* is the day for the Corinthians' relationship with God to be fully restored. Preachers usually apply 6:2 to non-Christians, but believers need to hear it as well, because salvation is a *process* of deliverance and transformation. In a sense, we have been saved (Romans 8:24), but we are also being saved (Philippians 2:12), and one day will be saved (Romans 13:11).

A good ambassador removes obstacles to reconciliation rather than creating them, and Paul is no exception (6:3). No one can fault him for doing anything to prevent others from coming to faith or to discredit the gospel. The undeniable characteristics of his ministry as God's servant commend him, so that he has no need to commend himself (6:4; see 4:2). If what Paul says resembles the self-commendation that he abhors (3:1–3; 11:16, 30), he must defend himself here or lose the Corinthians altogether. Often Christians rightly bear the pain of misunderstanding without self-defence, but when the truth of the gospel is at stake we do no one a favour by remaining silent.

The long series of twenty-eight phrases that follows in 6:4b–10 can be divided roughly into five sections. In the first section, three groups of three phrases show the truth of the first phrase—how Paul has exercised his ministry *with great endurance* (6:4b–5). He endured *external adversities* through various afflictions, hardships and calamities. He endured *persecution* from his fellow Jews and from Gentiles: beatings, imprisonments and riots, as the book of Acts confirms (Acts 16:22–23; 13:50; 14:19; 17:5; 19:23–41; 24:23–27; see 2 Corinthians 11:23–29). And he endured voluntarily *the cost of an itinerant ministry* that required him to work to support himself: labours, sleepless nights and hunger.

The second section emphasizes four of Paul's *ethical qualities* (6:6a). His motives are pure. He serves with knowledge—a grasp of God's word, rather than ignorant superstitions. He shows patience by suffering fools gladly, and acts in kindness toward the undeserving, two of the fruit produced by the Spirit (see Galatians 5:22).

That association of the latter qualities leads Paul to refer to the Holy Spirit (rather than the NRSV's 'holiness of spirit') in the following phrase which begins a third section of four *powers at work* in his ministry (6:6b–7a). Genuine (literally 'unhypocritical') love recalls Jesus' emphasis on love and his warnings against hypocrisy; for its power, see 5:14. Paul's 'true message' (a better translation) is effective for salvation (Romans 1:16), in contrast with the 'different gospel' the Corinthians are tempted to receive (11:4). The fourth point sums the section up: Paul serves by God's power.

A change of structure and a military image introduce a fourth section (6:7b–8a). Paul's ministry is a *spiritual battle* in which he wields righteous weaponry (see 1 Thessalonians 5:8; Ephesians 6:11–18). Soldiers typically carried a sword or spear with their *right* hand for offence and a shield in their *left* for defence. Whatever his 'scenario', whether held in honour or dishonour, in good repute or ill, Paul is prepared for his task.

The last section contrasts the way he and his companions are viewed from the outside with their inward reality (6:8b–10). Branded by some as deceivers, they are true. They may not be famous in society's eyes, but God knows them well. With Christ they are dying (see 4:11), yet live; punished often (11:24f), but not killed (Acts 14:19f). Despite grief in ministry (2:1–3), they rejoice (7:4, 7, 9). Although poor and having nothing, they bring great spiritual wealth to others and are heirs with Christ of everything (1 Corinthians 3:21f; see 2 Corinthians 8:9).

In his long digression about ministry, Paul has opened his heart fully and spoken freely. He hasn't withheld his strong feelings of affection for the Corinthians, although he feels that they have withheld support from him (6:11–12). Now he asks his spiritual children to respond to his open heart by opening theirs, so that the relationship may be fully restored (6:13).

Questions for thought

1. Which of the twenty-eight marks of Paul's ministry do you find most surprising? Which three do you think are the most important for effective ministry?

2. Try reading 6:3–10, replacing every 'we' with 'I'. We are not all called to be the apostle Paul (hallelujah!), but does this exercise suggest any realistic change you need to ask God's help for in your life?

Day 19

A PLEA for HOLINESS

2 Corinthians 6:14—7:1

This book assumes that Paul wrote these verses as part of 2 Corinthians, although the issue is disputed (see the Introduction). He has already used strong language to warn the Corinthians, back in 6:1, that they need to change. Paul's strong affection for them (6:11f; 7:1: 'beloved') now compels him to warn them further of the danger of peer pressure. 1 Corinthians reveals that some among the congregation were very immature believers. A number were still negatively influenced by their non-Christian background (1 Corinthians 15:32–33). We do not know the exact problem Paul addresses here, but his main point is clear: to be a Christian is to be holy. That involves, among other things, separation from certain relationships and activities.

Paul begins with a call not to be 'mismated' with unbelievers (6:14a). The word literally means 'unequally yoked', and is used in the Septuagint at Deuteronomy 22:10 to prohibit yoking together different kinds of animals. Here Paul could be referring to Christians marrying unbelievers (although he tells those who are already married to non-Christians not to seek a divorce, in 1 Corinthians 7:12–13), joining in close partnerships with them in business, consorting with immoral people (1 Corinthians 5:9–11), or sharing in religious meals in pagan temples. We know that he forbade the latter in 1 Corinthians 10:14–22.

The theologians Frances Young and David Ford suggest that Paul is thinking about apostasy. If the Corinthians refuse his appeal to be reconciled to God, if they reject Paul and pursue teachers who offer appealing substitutes instead of the true gospel (11:4), they will join those who perish (2:15; 4:3). Warnings of this strength to Christians appear elsewhere in Galatians 5:2, 4 and Hebrews 6:4–8; 10:26–31. Apostasy is a kind of spiritual adultery, so Paul urges them not to step back into conformity with the non-Christian world, but forward into holiness.

He supports that with a series of five rhetorical questions, each expecting the strong answer, 'No' (6:14b–16a). The righteousness that Christ died to create in them (5:21) has no partnership with lawlessness. There is no fellowship (the word means 'sharing') between light and darkness—otherwise one becomes the other. Christ doesn't harmonize (we get our word 'symphony' from this Greek word) with Beliar, another name for Satan. Likewise, one who trusts in Christ has a very different outlook on life from that of an unbeliever. To the Jews it is unthinkable that the temple of God might have any agreement with lifeless idols.

But that is precisely what Christians collectively are: the temple of the living God (6:16b). Paul has said this before in

1 Corinthians 3:16–17, and he implies it every time he reminds them that the Holy Spirit dwells within them (1 Corinthians 2:12; 6:19; 12:13; 2 Corinthians 1:22; 4:13; 5:5). That the one of whom angels cry, 'Holy, holy, holy' lives *in* us takes some getting used to!

Paul strings together several Old Testament quotations to develop the idea that the Corinthians are a temple and thus should not compromise themselves (6:16c–18). He combines Leviticus 26:11–12 and Ezekiel 37:26–27 to show that God dwells with them (6:16c). Isaiah 52:11 urged the Israelites to leave their place of exile in Babylon and return to the promised land; Paul uses the passage to call his hearers away from the lure of paganism in Corinth, adding a word of welcome from Ezekiel 20:34 (6:17). Finally he adapts 2 Samuel 7:8, 14 (adding the words 'and daughters'!) to stress the great privilege Christians have in their relationship as children to God their Father (6:18).

If these wonderful promises have any meaning, the Corinthians must share a family resemblance with their Father and be a fit dwelling place for God. Paul summarizes with an appeal for cleansing from whatever is defiling them and for continuing on to the goal of holiness in the fear of God (7:1; see 5:10–11). 'Holy' means 'set apart'; biblical holiness includes being set apart positively *for* God as well as negatively *from* that which he opposes. Like salvation, this is a process that has been begun (1 Corinthians 1:2), is continuing (1 Thessalonians 4:3) and will be completed (Ephesians 5:25f).

Unfortunately, for many 'holiness' connotes superiority rather than service, isolation from the world instead of transformation of it. Paul still fully expects believers to associate and eat with unbelievers (1 Corinthians 5:10; 10:27). If he thought holiness meant withdrawing from non-Christians he would never have had any converts! By contrast, true holiness is something beautiful and attractive, offering a lasting alternative to society's passing fads and fashions. Jesus *differed*. He could love people without approving their every attitude and activity.

Questions for thought

1. What does authentic holiness look like in our culture?

2. Is it possible to be holy and not judgmental? Is the idea of 'truth' intolerant?

3. What are the implications if we believe that the Christian community is a temple of God?

Day 20

A NEEDED REASSURANCE

2 Corinthians 7:2—4

After the warning to the Corinthians in 6:14—7:1, Paul returns to the subject of their relationship with him. Despite the implicit rebuke in what he has just said, he wants to assure them of his goodwill. Using a different word with a similar meaning to that in 6:13, he again asks them to make room in their hearts for him (7:2). There is no reason not to, because Paul has done nothing to alienate them (7:2b). He doesn't want to make them feel guilty, because he cares deeply for them and wants no separation (7:3). In fact, he's proud of them; they are a source of comfort and joy in his afflictions (7:4).

The three denials in 7:2 may well reflect accusations made against Paul, poisoning the attitude of some towards him. The tense of his verbs indicates that he's thinking of specific actions in the past. The word for 'wrong' here means to act unjustly and so to hurt another. Paul uses the word only a few verses later in 2 Corinthians to refer to the brother who had wronged him (7:12). Paul didn't do the wrong thing when he wrote to the Corinthians to discipline this man (7:8; see 2:1—11). In fact, some Corinthians had wronged each other by defrauding and going to court against one another (I Corinthians 6:7–8).

Second, he has 'corrupted' no one. This word means 'to ruin', and its use elsewhere three times in his letters to the Corinthians illustrates its different range of meanings. Divisive attitudes and actions can threaten to *destroy* the temple of God's people (I Corinthians 3:17). 'Bad company *corrupts* good morals'—a proverb Paul quotes to correct the Corinthians when they are conforming to their culture and denying the truth of resurrection (I Corinthians 15:33). Finally, they are in danger of turning away from Paul to follow others who would *lead astray* their minds (2 Corinthians 11:3).

Third, he has 'taken advantage' of no one. The word means to exploit, and is usually associated with greed (a related word appears in I Corinthians 5:10f; 6:10). Paul is seeking money from the Corinthians for the Jerusalem collection, and he wants at all costs to avoid any misconception about his motives (9:5; see 12:17–18).

Although Paul is referring to himself, each of these accusations could be made toward some of the Corinthians. But Paul isn't playing a game, and he quickly reassures them of his intention (7:3). He is seeking to clear himself, not to send them on a guilt trip! Unlike the ministry of condemnation (3:9), his is one of reconciliation. The last thing he wants is for the Corinthians to misunderstand yet again.

To stress that his motive is positive, Paul repeats the essence of what he has said before—they are in his heart (see 3:2; 6:11–12), even 'to die together and to live together'. These last words are part of a familiar expression of abiding friendship, loyalty and commitment (2 Samuel 15:21). Paul, however, reverses the normal order of 'living' and 'dying' because of his Christian expectation of life after death. He is committed to them 'through thick and thin'; as far as he is concerned, nothing will separate them.

In fact, Paul can speak with great freedom (*parresia*, see Day 11 on 3:12) towards the Corinthians and with unreserved goodwill (7:4). He boasts freely of them to others, no doubt largely about what God has done in their lives. Filled with encouragement (*paraklesis*, see Day 2 on 1:3–7), he 'superabounds' (the literal meaning of the verb) with joy in his afflictions when he thinks of them. How quickly Paul moves to heights of passion as he expresses his strength of feeling!

These are not empty words of flattery, carefully crafted to manipulate the hearers to effect a particular response. Paul has good reason to feel this way, especially given the good news Titus has brought (7:6–7, 13). His words are the heartfelt overflow that comes from someone who has prayed and continues to pray daily at length for a group of people, so that in spite of their failures and flaws, they are his *family*. Like a good father, Paul communicates his love and withholds no good thing from them.

Questions for thought

1. Our motivations for speaking are just as important as the things we say, if not more so. What motivates the things you typically say?

2. What forms do injustice, corruption and exploitation take in the Church today?

3. What kinds of actions are appropriate to reassure people of our love and care for them, when we have disagreements with them?

Day 21

TWO GRIEFS OBSERVED

2 Corinthians 7:5–11

Paul now explains how the Corinthians have brought him consolation and overflowing joy in all his afflictions (see 7:4). His account picks up the trail of events he stopped recounting in 2:13, before his long digression about ministry (2:14—7:4). In the midst of Paul's hardship in Macedonia, Titus arrived, bringing encouraging news (7:5–7). As a result, Paul doesn't regret the grief he caused the Corinthians with his severe letter (2:3–4), because it has provoked a positive response (7:8–11).

When Paul arrived in Macedonia after his journey from Troas he was thrown in at the deep end of suffering with the believers there (7:5; see 8:1–2). Whether his fears included himself (as 1 Corinthians 2:3 could be taken to suggest), or more probably concern for the Macedonians, for Titus and for how the Corinthians would respond to his letter (2:13), Paul felt anxious and inadequate in himself. The Corinthians also experienced a fear (translated 'alarm' in 7:11, but the same Greek word) that mobilized them to action. In both cases, God proved faithful.

God brought encouragement, comforting those who were low (7:6–7). Again Paul repeatedly uses the same Greek root (NRSV: 'console/consolation') found so often in 1:3–7 and throughout this letter. Titus, no doubt anxious about the Corinthians' situation, was encouraged by their threefold response (7:7): they longed to see Paul and for restoration of their relationship, they mourned (a very strong word, used elsewhere in the New Testament only at Matthew 2:18) having caused him such pain, and they were zealous on behalf of the apostle they had spurned. Paul was doubly encouraged, both by seeing Titus again and by hearing the good news he brought, leading to more joy.

The severe letter had worked. Paul's rebuke shocked the Corinthians into doing what they should have done long before—taking disciplinary action against the offending brother (see the Introduction). The apostle's letter grieved them (the same Greek word meaning 'to cause pain' in 2:2, 4), but in a healthy way (7:8–9).

Like a loving parent disciplining a child, Paul had mixed feelings about the process. At the time, he regretted *having* to grieve the Corinthians with his rebuke. But he doesn't regret doing so, because it was necessary for their benefit and had a good outcome. The church wasn't harmed at all, though they could have been, had Paul handled the situation poorly. His ability to exercise long-distance discipline successfully says a great deal about his character and integrity. 'Faithful are the wounds of a friend...' (Proverbs 27:6, AV).

Paul distinguishes between two kinds of grief (7:10). 'Godly' grief is a sorrow for mistakes that prompts us to *repent*, that is, to turn away from wrong attitudes and behaviour. This is a constructive pain that ultimately results in reconciliation; it is a part of the process of our salvation. There are no regrets with this grief because it leads us not just to recognize but also to deal with the mistakes of the past, and to take action, where possible and appropriate, to rectify the problem. This grief is *brief* (7:8), because by God's grace, it works to *transform* the situation.

On the other hand, 'worldly' grief is the sorrow simply of having been found out, the sorrow of failure, resentment and bitterness. It refuses to change, and therefore it lasts. Rather than turning outward to God, it curls inward on self, and can lead to deepening depression (which is often caused by anger at ourselves), self-destruction and even death. It is the remorse of Judas. Self-pity leads nowhere but darkness.

Among the Corinthians, godly grief produced an eagerness and intense commitment to clear themselves by doing the right thing (7:11). Vexation and alarm at what they had done to Paul gave way to longing and zeal for Paul, and the discipline that was needed. Summing up their response, Paul uses the same language in Greek to describe the Corinthians that he has earlier used of himself, although most English translations miss this. Just as his behaviour *commended* his ministry by his *purity* (6:6), so their actions *proved* them now to be *guiltless* in response to that very authority they had questioned.

Questions for thought

1. Someone has said that fear is the opposite of faith. Do you agree? Why or why not?

2. There are other kinds of grief (such as the grief of bereavement) besides the two alternatives that Paul describes here; his purpose is not to discuss grief in general. What experiences of 'godly' grief and pain have you suffered, and how have they changed you?

3. What can the Church do to help people who suffer from 'worldly' grief?

Day 22

'TIDINGS of COMFORT & JOY'

2 Corinthians 7:12–16

In this passage, Paul concludes his discussion of the recent crisis over church discipline which occasioned his severe letter. Seeking to encourage the Corinthians with praise, he re-emphasizes his *comfort* (7:13; that same word as consolation in 7:4, 6–7) and *joy* (7:13, 16; see 7:4, 7, 9), giving two specific reasons. First, Paul's ultimate purpose for that letter—to cause the church to rediscover their own commitment to him as God's apostle—was fulfilled (7:12–13a). Second, he was delighted because of Titus's joy when the Corinthians proved Paul's confidence about them to be well-founded (7:13b–16).

In the ancient world, when Jewish writers wanted to stress the greater importance of one thing over another, they would sometimes express it by saying essentially 'this, not that'. So, when the prophet declared, 'I desire steadfast love and not sacrifice' (Hosea 6:6), he was not intending to deny the value of sacrifice, but to emphasize the priority of love. When Jesus said it was necessary to 'hate' our fathers and mothers to be his disciple (Luke 14:26), he was not contradicting the commandment to honour parents (Luke 18:20), but stressing the even greater priority of loving and obeying him (see Matthew 10:37). Likewise, Paul in 7:12 is not intending to deny that he wrote his severe letter on behalf of the two people directly involved in the problem. Rather, he states what was a more fundamental reason for the letter, which he now sees clearly in hindsight. What was really at stake was the relationship of an entire congregation and their leader.

Paul does not identify who did wrong, nor who was wronged.

The Corinthians certainly knew, but we have to guess (see the Introduction and notes on Day 6). Most commentators agree that, given his statements in 2:1, 5 and 13:2, Paul was the hurt party referred to here; apparently he was publicly challenged by someone to offer proof that Christ was speaking through him (13:3), and the rest of the church sat back and failed to support the apostle. Their commitment to Paul had seemed to evaporate because they lacked the courage to take a stand with him in a confrontation. They preferred to watch from the safety of the sidelines, forgetting their accountability to God. Paul's severe letter caused them to search their hearts and to rediscover their former 'zeal' (literally 'eagerness'; see 7:11; 8:7) for him. His risky strategy worked, and the Corinthians learned something important about themselves. Sometimes it takes a sharp shock to show us what matters most to us.

Most English translations recognize a shift in thought starting in 7:13b and so they begin a new paragraph there. Paul finds a second cause of encouragement and joy in the resulting change in Titus. Like Paul, his mind had raced with thoughts about the risk taken by the severe letter; he too wondered what sort of reception he would receive when he arrived in Corinth on Paul's behalf (7:13). Although hurt by them, Paul risked further humiliation by expressing more pride and confidence in the Corinthians than Titus thought they deserved (7:14). A faith-full pastor is typically more hopeful than the 'realists' in a congregation think the situation merits! But the Corinthians came to their senses, Paul's 'boasting' in them proved true, and Titus's anxiety has now turned into joy, to Paul's further delight (7:13b).

Memories feed the springs of joy. Recalling the welcome received and the Corinthians' obedience causes Titus to be moved all the more deeply in his affection for them (7:15). Likewise, remembering God's grace to us in the past, recounting his blessings, can fundamentally change our perspective on the present. When people stop remembering the good, grumbling sneaks in and stifles joy.

A final observation concerns Paul's pastoral strategy. Notice his statement about the 'obedience of *all*' of the Corinthians (7:15) and his rejoicing because of his 'complete confidence' in them (7:16; the Greek means 'courage in every way'). This seems far different from the very critical tone Paul will eventually assume in parts of chapters 10–13. Although many scholars claim that those chapters belong to a separate, subsequent letter (see the Introduction), we should not underestimate Paul's capacity to praise and to confront in the same letter. As a pastor, Paul is working hard in chapter 7 to encourage the Corinthians, just as they have encouraged him. They are certainly not perfect, and problems still remain, but as a good pastor, Paul knows the importance of identifying, naming and exulting in instances of transforming grace in his friends, as he seeks to urge them forward into the image of Christ.

Questions for thought

1. The Church today is experiencing conflict over a number of crucial issues. In what ways do Christians 'watch from the safety of the sidelines' today? What issues do you need to take a stand on before God? How should you go about doing that?

2. Are there any steps you can take to help you remember more often God's grace to you in the past?

3. How do you think the Corinthians felt when they read this passage? Why?

Day 23

THOSE

AMAZING MACEDONIANS

---

2 Corinthians 8:1–5

Chapters 8–9 are an attempt to persuade the Corinthians to fulfil their pledge to contribute to the collection Paul planned to take back with him for the church in Jerusalem (1 Corinthians 16:1ff; Romans 15:2ff; see the Introduction). Here is a chance to see a first-century apostolic fund-raiser at work; his strategy invites comparison with practices today. Most importantly, our text reminds us of what grace (*charis*, used five times in the first nine verses) looks like in action.

First of all, in 8:1–5 Paul emphasizes *the example of the Macedonians*—that is, the Christians to the north, in Philippi, Thessalonica and Beroea (see the map on page 6). 'We want you to know... about the grace of God that has been granted...'

Paul frequently used the language of example. He knew that Christian character is as much caught as taught, and his letters are full of references to people who are good at this or that. Examples put flesh and bone on truth. They offer powerful motivations to act, sometimes far more powerful incentives than an immediate appeal.

Paul's strategy here is to inspire and evoke a godly jealousy (there was some hostility between Macedonians and the Greeks to the south), and, when appropriate, to shame his hearers—but without going for the jugular. A good example is a strong argument. And the Macedonians weren't just good, they were great. The secret was grace. Grace turned them into givers who overflowed in a wealth of generosity.

Paul tells us ten things about their giving. He states three of them in verse 2:

1. They gave *in a time of great affliction* (NRSV, 'severe ordeal of affliction', literally 'much testing with pressure'). We don't know the nature of the pressures they suffered (probably arising because of their faith), but their affliction, like Paul's, didn't distract them from the needs of others.

2. They gave *with abundant joy* that overflowed ('abundant' and 'overflowed' come from the same family of words in Greek). This kind of irrepressible joy (in people whose lives were full of trouble) was a striking feature of early Christianity.

3. They gave *in extreme poverty* (literally, 'down to the depth'/rock-bottom poverty). Poverty didn't extinguish Christian joy or prevent generosity. Those who have very little are often the most carefree of souls—and the most generous.

The long sentence running through verses 3–6 gives us seven more points about the Macedonians' giving. The order of the Greek text is a little different from our English versions:

4. They gave *according to and even beyond their means.* In other words, they gave more than what was comfortable and affordable. Like the widow's giving in the temple (Mark 12:41ff), they offered a *sacrifice.* Paul adds, 'I testify'—a holy version of 'I swear'—because he knows that what he says is hard to believe.

5. They gave *voluntarily*, literally 'of their own choice'. They were responding to no strong-arm tactics, no high-pressure sell, no command from Paul, no spiritual blackmail. The Macedonians were like Zacchaeus, whose immediate instinct, because of the grace he experienced with Jesus, was *freely* to give to others.

6. They *saw giving as a privilege.* Do you know *anyone* who thinks that way? The Greek text says 'they begged us with much

urging, for the *favour'* (there's that word *grace* again) of sharing in ministry for the saints. Normally the fund-raisers are the ones who do the asking; Chrysostom marvelled that it was the Macedonians, not Paul, who did the begging.

7. They *saw it as sharing in ministry*. Sharing is *koinonia*—fellowship—not simply talk over coffee or in a home-group, but a tangible giving of stuff. Paul wanted his people to see that their use of money is a ministry. This is the kind of every-member ministry every vicar would love to see!

8. They gave *unexpectedly*. They surprised Paul. This is the essence of grace. Part of the attractiveness of Jesus was that people kept finding themselves surprised. Surprising giving is powerful when you experience it. When a community stops surprising people, it's stopped living by grace.

9. They *gave themselves first to Christ*. Without this step, giving becomes only a duty or burden. Giving themselves first to Christ was the preventative medicine that helped the Macedonians avoid what someone has called *cirrhosis of the giver* (an acute condition which renders the patient's hand immovable when it is appropriate to move it in the direction of the wallet or purse. One treatment is to remove the patient from the church, since it is clinically observable that this condition does not occur in other places such as the supermarket, restaurant, or theatre).

10. They *made themselves available as well as their money*. They placed themselves at the apostle's disposal, which meant, for some of them, travelling with Paul to safeguard the collection money. Acts gives us some of their names—people like Sopater of Beroea, Aristarchus and Secundus of Thessalonica, and Epaphroditus of Philippi. Grace had turned takers into givers.

Questions for thought

1. Why is it that those who can barely scrape by on what they have are frequently the first ones to offer help to someone in need?

2. What experiences in your life have made you want to respond by giving?

3. Have you discovered the joy of *surprising* giving?

Day 24

GIVING *that* EXCELS

---

2 Corinthians 8:6–9

In verses 6–8 Paul appeals to *the excellence of the Corinthians.* As a result of the stunning generosity of the Macedonians, Paul has urged Titus to go to Corinth to help motivate them to complete their grace gift, and Paul uses that word *charis* again to link the Corinthians with their northern neighbours.

Again he reminds them of what they have received, *by grace.* Like the Macedonians, the Corinthians *excel* (the same Greek word in verse 7, meaning 'to overflow' or 'abound', that he used back in verse 2); only they excel in faith, speech and knowledge. Paul used these last two words in 1 Corinthians 1:5 when he said, 'In every way you have been enriched in Christ, in speech and knowledge of every kind'—probably references to spiritual gifts emphasized by the Corinthians. The reference to faith likewise probably recalls things like the gifts of healing and miraculous powers that are linked to faith in 1 Corinthians 12:9–10. The Corinthians also excel in eagerness and in love, although Paul's expression here means either 'our love for you' (as the NRSV has it) or 'the love that had its beginning in us but now is in you'.

This is good pastoral strategy because it focuses first on what God has done and is doing. Good teaching spots and names grace at work. That's ground for rejoicing and praising God. It promotes *thankfulness* for what *is* and *expectancy* for what *can be* rather than *complaining* about what *is not*.

The Corinthians are rich in lots of ways, and the logic is irresistible: 'Since you excel in those ways… excel also in this grace gift.'

Paul is careful in what he says. In the Greek, he doesn't use a direct imperative here. And in the next verse, he makes it clear that he isn't giving an apostolic order. Instead, he's testing (a word related to that used of the Macedonians' testing in verse 2) the genuineness of the Corinthians' love by comparing it with the Macedonians' eagerness (NRSV says 'earnestness' but it's the same word used in verse 7). This 'testing' word does not mean testing with a view to failure, but testing with a view to success (see 2:9 and the comments in Day 6).

There must have been a smile on the face of his secretary when Paul dictated verse 8. He's sailing close to the wind. The comparison is out in the open now. He's trying to motivate them by some friendly competition. But Paul hasn't lumbered the Corinthians with a load of 'oughts', 'musts', 'need tos' and 'shoulds', that pepper too many sermons and smother the flame of grace. It's hard to argue with the generosity of God and with the desire to show the genuineness of our profession.

It's even harder to argue with the *exchange of Christ's riches for poverty* in verse 9. The Corinthians know from experience the grace (translated 'generous act' in the NRSV, but it's *charis* again) of the Lord Jesus. The one who was rich in pre-incarnate glory and status became poor for their sake (the words, 'for your sakes' are emphatic) in order to enrich the Corinthians by his poverty.

Regardless of physical resources, Christians are rich, and shall be richer; unfortunately we sometimes lose sight of that. Paul knew that remembering what we have makes a difference (Ephesians 1:18). To name a few jewels from this letter, we have the down-payment and guarantee of the Spirit (1:22; 5:5), the potential of daily renewal (4:16), an eternal weight of glory

(4:18), an eternal house in heaven (5:1), unending fellowship with Christ (5:8), a new creation (5:17), reconciliation (5:18), righteousness (5:21); the list goes on and on.

When people know the riches in Christ that can't be taken from them, they start to loosen that death grip on the things that promise but can't really provide security. To paraphrase Jim Elliot, one of the five US missionaries martyred in Ecuador in the 1950s, 'They are no fools who give what they cannot keep to gain what they cannot lose.'

Questions for thought

1. In what ways does your life abound or excel? How does that affect the way you relate to other people?

2. Would it ever be appropriate for Christians to 'compete' in giving today? If so, how?

3. What people give is a measure of their own sense of security. What makes your life secure?

Day 25

FINISHING RESPONSIBLY

2 Corinthians 8:10–15

At last an *exhortation to finish what was begun* clearly emerges in verses 10–11. Again Paul urges his advice, but he doesn't command like a Roman emperor. What is appropriate is that people *carry through* with what they say they will do.

The NRSV in verses 10–11 doesn't make it so clear, but Paul is reminding the Corinthians that they expressed their eagerness to contribute a year ago. In two ways they were actually *ahead* of the Macedonians: the Corinthians had the desire to help first, and they had made a start when Titus was with them earlier. But instead of laying up an amount every week as Paul had suggested in I Corinthians 16, they hadn't acted on their good intentions. They meant well, but just didn't get around to it.

Carrying through with commitments is one of the hardest things to achieve in a culture that encourages us to pamper ourselves. Fulfilling the ideas and impulses of the Spirit to give becomes particularly difficult if we delay action. The longer we wait to carry out a generous act, especially if it will really cost us something, the easier it is to find reasons not to do it.

Paul concludes his appeal in 11–15 with *expectations for responsible giving*. They challenge and scare, but they also reassure. If people take what Paul says seriously, it will revolutionize their giving. But it also helps to ensure that giving is responsible and realistic.

First, notice what Paul does not say. There is no mention of the tithe or ten per cent. Despite the Old Testament precedents about tithing for the Levites, the only reference to the practice in the New Testament is what Jesus says about Pharisees tithing herbs while neglecting weightier matters of the law. Christians will want to give far more than a tenth, but there is no law here for us.

Second, the amount to give is *according to one's means* (8:11). In other words, God doesn't expect what is impossible for people to give; he doesn't call them to carry continually a burden of guilt for poverty that is beyond their capacity to respond to. The news media remind us daily of staggering needs around the world. With knowledge comes responsibility, but we are only called to do what God enables us to do.

Third, in verse 12 he makes the point that *the amount is not as important as the eagerness*. Giving is *in proportion* to one's ability. This doesn't mean a fixed percentage for everyone—that would cripple those on a fixed income, and leave the wealthy to live in untroubled luxury—but a sum 'in keeping with' what each of us has. As Jesus said, 'From everyone who has been given much, much will be demanded' (Luke 12:48). We will say more about the *attitude* of the giver when we look at 9:6ff on Day 28.

Fourth, in 13–15, we see that *the goal is equality in respect to basic needs*, as supported by the quotation from the gathering of manna in Exodus 16. That means that *normally*, Christians give out of their surplus, but not out of what they need for their basic existence. The Macedonians' act of giving to the Jerusalem collection, like that of the widow in the gospels who gave all that she had to the temple, was an *exception*, not the rule. Paul doesn't want the Corinthians to feel pressured to give so much away that they become a burden on others. That wouldn't help.

Fifth, Paul wants for the Corinthians a *humility* in giving, with the awareness that they will *receive* from their Jerusalem brethren as well as give to them (8:14). When giving is one-sided it becomes patronizing, encouraging an unhealthy one-way dependency. Affluent Christians today in the West have just as much to learn from believers in the Two-Thirds World as they have to contribute.

One way we can work toward the goal of equality for all is to forgive our debts, as we have been forgiven our debts by God. As we see enormous economic inequities among the nations intensified by escalating and unpayable Two-Thirds World debts to the world bank, more and more Christians are calling for a Jubilee year, in which these debts are substantially reduced or written off altogether. In addition, we can think more creatively about how to get our surplus to those people for whom it will do the most good.

Questions for thought

1. Are there any commitments you have made that you need to fulfil now?

2. What is the difference between Paul's vision for Christian charity and socialism?

3. What specific, realistic and responsible steps can Christians take today to respond to economic problems such as Two-Thirds World debt, or the plight of homeless people on our streets?

A FIRST-CENTURY SECURICOR

2 Corinthians 8:16–24

Some people are hesitant to contribute to those who solicit for charities because they wonder whether their money will ever get back to the charity. Paul's point in 8:16–24 is to assure the Corinthians that the team who will handle and transport their contribution for the Jerusalem collection is trustworthy. He introduces the three people who will be coming to Corinth, bringing the letter we know as 2 Corinthians with them. Here we see Paul's concern to ensure that all financial arrangements are completely clear and without cause for suspicion.

In 1 Corinthians, Paul had already taken two precautions for the Jerusalem collection. He told the church to collect the money before he arrived (1 Corinthians 16:2), so that he would not be involved in the process. Second, he invited them to appoint their own people to accompany the gift on to Jerusalem (1 Corinthians 16:3), so that there would be no uncertainty about its safe delivery.

Now he writes a commendation of the three-man team he is sending. The leader of the group will be Titus, who shares Paul's eagerness (*spoude*, sometimes translated 'zeal'; an important theme in this section) for the Corinthians (8:16). Although he had only recently returned to Paul in Macedonia, when the apostle asked him to go, he was more than ready to do so voluntarily (8:17; see 7:13–15). The verbs translated 'is going' in 8:17 and 'are sending' in 8:18, 22 are actually in the past tense, even though Titus's trip is yet to take place when Paul dictates the letter. This indicates that Titus was probably the bearer of this letter, and that Paul is speaking from the point of view of those who received the letter in Corinth.

Paul does not state the name of the other two men who are coming with Titus. Obviously Titus will introduce them when he brings and reads this letter. One of them is famous for his work in relation to the gospel, but the nature of that work is unstated; the text says literally, 'whose praise in the gospel (is) throughout all the churches' (8:18). Early interpreters thought this to be Luke, but there are many other possibilities, including Sopater, Aristarchus or Secundus, Macedonians who accompanied Paul (Acts 20:4).

In any case, this brother was appointed *by the churches* to travel with Paul and to help with the collection, a point that leads Paul to underscore that this project is completely 'above board' in its intentions (8:19–21). The Greek word translated 'generous gift' in 8:19 is *charis* again ('grace'), a reminder that Christian giving is a *response* to the grace of God that has already come to us. The collection is for the Lord's glory and praise (not Paul's), and to show the goodwill of the participants, mostly Gentile churches, to their Jewish Christian brothers and sisters in Jerusalem (8:19). A great deal of money is involved, and Paul is determined to avoid any semblance of impropriety (8:20), so he and his colleagues are giving thought beforehand to what is right both in the sight of God and of other people (8:21). Would that all church projects kept this twofold concern in mind!

The second unnamed brother is called 'our' brother (8:22) in contrast to 'the' brother (8:18), an indication that this person is a regular travelling companion of Paul and known to the Corinthians (see 12:18). He is reliable and well-proven, having been tested often. Keen in many respects, like Titus he is all the more *eager* to come and help administer the collection because of his confidence (the Greek text does not specify whose confidence, but the context favours this brother's) in the Corinthians. Titus' enthusiasm obviously rubbed off on others as well as on Paul, as he recounted his visit to Corinth.

Paul summarizes his team in 8:23 before appealing to the Corinthians to receive them in a worthy fashion (8:24). As Paul's partner (*koinonos*, from the root meaning 'fellowship' or 'sharing') and co-worker, Timothy's credentials are impeccable (8:22a). Sent by the churches as their representatives and messengers, the two other brothers are 'the glory of Christ'. By this last phrase Paul probably means that they are at work to bring glory to *Christ* through their ministries and through the collection they serve (see 8:19). How the church in Corinth receives them will therefore demonstrate to the other churches the Corinthians' true character (8:24). Paul wants those churches to hear of love in action (see 8:8), meaning not only hospitality but co-operation with the team by fulfilling their pledges to the collection. And just as in the case of his boasts to Titus (7:14), he wants his boasts to the churches about the Corinthians to prove true.

Questions for thought

1. How is good administration a form of pastoral care?

2. What wise financial practices can you find in this passage?

3. Organizing collective efforts between churches is sometimes complicated and hard work. Is it really worth it?

Day 27

PREPARATION BEATS HUMILIATION!

2 Corinthians 9:1–5

Some scholars are puzzled by Paul's return to the subject of the collection after what looks like closing remarks in 8:23–24. They think that chapter 9 must belong to another letter. But the chapter is not lacking in any Greek manuscripts, and Paul has good reason to say more to motivate the Corinthians to finish what they promised. The purpose of 9:1–5 is to explain why he has decided to send Titus and the brothers *ahead of himself*. Paul fully intends to visit Corinth again (12:14; 13:1) and to accompany the collection on its way to Jerusalem. The reason he is sending the three-man team first is to ensure that everything is in order when he arrives in Corinth with his other travelling companions.

Verses 1–2 are a good example of how to remind others to do something without insulting their intelligence or intentions; we do that every time when we say, 'I know I don't need to say this, but...' Paul expresses his confidence that he knows the Corinthians' attitude towards giving to the collection, so that he really doesn't have to write to them about it—but he does anyway, reflecting the care he takes to ensure that things won't go wrong (see also Philippians 3:1; 1 Thessalonians 4:9). He sees the gift as a 'ministry' (9:1; see 8:4) for the Jerusalem 'saints', Paul's characteristic way of referring to Christians (see 1:1).

Precisely because of his confidence in the Corinthians, Paul has gone out on a limb in his praise of them (9:2). He knows their 'eagerness' to give, a word already used of them in 8:11, 12 (also translated 'goodwill' in 8:19). His parental pride has led him to boast to the Macedonians about the Corinthians' readiness to give since last year. Paul has created a sort of friendly competition (see 8:8 and the comments in Day 24), so that the Corinthians' zeal has provoked many of the Macedonians to the kind of generosity already described in 8:1–5.

Although Paul is confident, he knows he can take nothing for granted, particularly since he has heard that the project has stalled in Corinth. The Corinthians have been enthusiastic about giving *in principle*, but they haven't got around to doing it fully yet. If the gift isn't fully collected when Paul and his companions arrive, along with at least three Macedonians (see Acts 20:2–6), both he and the Corinthians will be humiliated (9:3–4). Being treated in a humiliating way for the sake of Christ is one thing, but the humiliation of having their word proven untrue is quite another.

It's hard to overestimate the importance of keeping your word in the ancient world. More so than today, words had power and carried responsibility; if what Paul said God was doing through the Corinthians didn't prove true, it would undermine the apostle's credibility and authority with the Macedonians and other churches represented by his companions, and thereby undermine his gospel. It could be said that Paul has got himself into this fix in the first place by excessive optimism! However, Paul isn't naïve in his boasting about the Corinthians; rather, as a wise pastor he has chosen to emphasize the positive. The Corinthians have made promises too. Paul knows that they are a proud bunch, and he shrewdly appeals to that pride by reminding them of the shame they will bring upon themselves if they do not carry out their promise (9:4–5).

Therefore Titus and co. are coming early to ensure that their readiness is complete (9:3) and that the collection is fully prepared before Paul and the rest arrive (9:5). The words 'bountiful gift' and 'voluntary gift' in 9:5 are the same word in Greek, *eulogia*, or 'blessing'. The word translated 'extortion' normally means 'greed'; it could refer to the way the gift is secured ('an extortion', NRSV) or to the spirit in which it is given ('as grudgingly given', NIV). The next paragraph favours the latter interpretation. Paul wants the gift to be a true blessing freely given, not a last minute token given grudgingly.

Questions for thought

1. Paul planned ahead here and took action to avoid a disgrace. Some people are planners by nature; others at the other end of the spectrum emphasize spontaneity. In what areas should Christians today plan ahead and anticipate alternatives?

2. When, if ever, do you think it is appropriate to 'boast' about what other Christians are doing?

3. Paul assumes here that people have a sense of shame. Do you think that shame is still a part of life today? If so, where? Is it ever a legitimate motivation for behaviour?

DAY 28

The HARVEST *of* GENEROSITY (i)

---

2 Corinthians 9:6–9

Here Paul begins his most compelling argument for giving. He doesn't appeal to the poverty of the recipients of the gift, as so many modern fundraisers do. Instead, he points his hearers to the positive benefits of generosity, calling for genuine cheer in giving and showing why that is appropriate. There is good reason for giving gladly, because those who do so participate in a divine economy that overflows to the praise and glory of God.

Paul begins by stating a farmer's truth with which there is no argument: how much a person sows determines how much they will reap (9:6). By itself, this principle would encourage giving simply as a calculated means in order to get. We find that teaching today in the 'prosperity gospel' preached by some. A radio evangelist in America once announced, 'Send us $20 and God will give you back three times what you give us.' He received a letter from a listener telling him, 'Why don't you send us the $20 and you'll receive what *you* need three times over'! As we shall see, Paul's point is not what individual sowers will reap *for themselves*. Rather, God will provide, so that people can give bountifully (literally, 'with blessings'; see Day 27 on 9:5) in the assurance that they will enable a harvest for all, to his praise.

Verse 7 is one of the few direct 'commands' Paul gives to his readers in chapters 8–9. He has already implied that our attitude in giving is more important than the amount (8:12); now it becomes explicit. Each should contribute just as they have decided in their heart, not grudgingly (literally 'out of pain') or under compulsion (literally 'of necessity'). Paul knows the Corinthians made their original decision to give with eagerness and enthusiasm (8:11; 9:2). That same gladness should be their attitude as they complete their promise, because God loves a 'cheerful' giver (the root from which we derive our word 'hilarious', see Romans 12:8). Here Paul echoes the text of Proverbs 22:9a, which says (only in the Septuagint): 'God blesses a cheerful and giving person.' When Paul says 'loves' in this case, he is not implying that God's love is conditional; the idea is that God 'approves' or 'esteems' such a person.

Scholars have characterized the economy of the ancient world as one of 'limited good', in the sense that people believed the total amount of wealth and resources available to be unchanging. There was no thought of a 'growth' economy in which everyone's standard of living could improve. The vast majority (including Paul) had little surplus of goods; subsistence was the best people could hope for. Those who gave to others expected a reciprocal act of equal value, otherwise this equilibrium would be upset and the giver's future endangered.

Paul explodes this picture of 'limited good' in 9:9. His is a vision of a divine 'economy' lived out by Christians, an economy which is ever experiencing an influx of grace from a God who gives in abundance. The little words 'God is able' puts it in a nutshell. Five times in this one verse Paul uses the Greek root translated 'all' or 'every' to emphasize that divine ability. God has the power to make *every* blessing (*charis*, 'grace' again) abound to the Corinthians, for the purpose that *always* having *all* sufficiency in *every* circumstance, they may abound in *every* good work. That's a fairly robust programme of enablement!

The words 'having enough' in 9:8 (NRSV) translate *autarkeia*, a term used by the Stoics to describe an ideal (to their way of thinking) state of self-sufficiency in isolation from others. Many people in the West seek that state today. Paul, however, takes this word and gives it a new meaning. He describes a state in which we become channels through which God's abundance flows richly to others. Rather than promoting an ever-voracious consumer economy, God's grace enables this kind of sufficiency, of having enough (see Philippians 4:12–13), so that, as the NRSV helpfully translates, 'you may *share* abundantly' in every good work.

Paul supports that notion of a cheerful giver who shares abundantly with a quotation from the Septuagint (9:9; Psalm

112:9). The last phrase of the quotation sounds as though it is referring to God. In fact, this psalm celebrates the blessedness of the one who fears the Lord and obeys him. The ambiguity may be intentional; in any event, there is a family likeness. Like his or her heavenly Father, this person sows widely and generously, gives to the poor, and their righteousness (seen in generosity) remains forever.

I know of a couple who decided they would begin giving more to God each year. They gradually built up their gifts to ten per cent of their gross income, but didn't stop there. The next year they increased the percentage, and so on, until eventually they were able to give over half of their income to others, yet they lived as well as anyone, despite the fact that they were on missionaries' salaries. They couldn't have begun by giving half a salary away. God provided a heart to give, honoured the first small steps they took, and gave them grace to take bigger steps. Their giving touched the lives of so many people that others began to give more too. In the process, they reaped much because they sowed much, and found a new freedom in cheerful giving.

Questions for thought

1. Paul believed in a God of abundance, overflow and extravagant grace. What can Christians do to foster that same character in their community's life, work and worship?

2. What prevents people from giving 'cheerfully'?

3. What are you currently sowing?

Day 29

The HARVEST
of GENEROSITY (ii)

2 Corinthians 9:10–15

In these verses Paul spells out what he has just said in 9:8–9, going on in the following verses to motivate the Corinthians to give, by reminding them of its wonderful effects. He likens his hearers to the righteous one from the quotation in Psalm 112 (9:10). God is at work providing throughout the process of producing bread, from its beginning in sowing to its final completion in a loaf (an echo of Isaiah 55:10). This same provider will enable and extend the blessing that is the collection. Using the language of Hosea 10:12, Paul says God will both supply and multiply what the Corinthians have to give (by making their gifts go far towards helping the Jewish-Christians in Jerusalem). He will also increase the harvest of their righteousness, not in the sense that the harvest *is* their increasing righteousness, but referring to the results from their righteous act of giving. In other words, grace has a ripple effect.

When people give in God's will, *everyone* wins (9:11–14). First, *the givers will benefit*. The Greek text makes it clear that when Paul says that the Corinthians will be enriched in every way 'for' their generosity, he does not mean *as a reward for* but *for the purpose of* their contributing (9:11a). He is not promising a kickback to be hoarded, but surpassing grace to enable giving all the more (9:14). Paul knows that people who have something to give often need a divine 'jump-start' to do so! This is the sort of enrichment everyone can use, regardless of their material wealth. Generosity is a sign of grace already given.

The givers will also benefit by effectively proving their character (9:13), since the ministry of the collection is another test for the Corinthians (see 2:9; 8:8). Their response to the needs of their Christian brothers and sisters will show their obedience to the confession they've made of faith in Christ. Furthermore, they will be prayed for by the Jerusalem saints (9:14; see Day 2 on 1:11), having established a much closer relationship with them through the gift.

The Corinthians' generosity in turn means that *the recipients will benefit*. Obviously, the collection will supply physical needs (9:12). It's a tangible expression of *fellowship* (koinonia, the word translated 'sharing' in 8:4 and 9:13). The gift will also cause the Jerusalem saints to speak to God, which is an exercise of faith. They will of course thank God (9:11b, 12) with a thanksgiving produced *through* Paul and his companions, inasmuch as they will be bringing the gift to Jerusalem. They will also now 'long' for the Corinthians with more than simply the knowledge that they exist (9:14).

Finally, through the giving, *God will be glorified*. He will be praised by the saints who will thank him for the gift (9:11–12). He will be glorified because of the obedience of Paul's hearers and their generosity (9:13); the Greek text is ambiguous as to who is glorifying God here, but in any case both groups would do so. The word 'ministry' in 9:12 is *leitourgia* (the root of our English word 'liturgy'), a term referring to service in a worship setting. Paul sees the collection itself as an act of service to God, so he and his companions are joining in to give him glory.

As Paul ponders how the grace at work in the collection could benefit all and bring glory to God, he can't help but break out in praise to the provider for the third time in this letter (9:15; 2:14; 8:16). He doesn't choose the usual verb for thanks (*eucharisteo*) but the noun *charis* ('grace') which we have seen so often and just previously in 9:14. 'Indescribable' in its wonder is God's gift of Christ (see 8:9). His obedience in becoming poor has made it possible for the Corinthians to become rich. Now it is their turn to reflect his glory.

It may strike us as odd that Paul went on at such length about a matter of finances. Money is something of a taboo subject in many Christian circles. This may be due to any number of reasons, including culture, suspicion of motives, or a sense of guilt. Yet it's striking how frequently Jesus mentioned the issue. If the frequency of sayings about money in the gospels is anything to go on, he taught something about it almost every other day (or in every other saying); he knew money was interesting and how its use is a barometer of the soul. So did Paul.

Judging by Paul's words in a later letter from Corinth (Romans 15:26), the apostle was successful in motivating his hearers to give. The degree of that success, however, remains unknown.

Questions for thought

1. Why is thanksgiving so important to Paul?

2. What does the word 'fellowship' mean to you? In what tangible ways can Christians express it today?

3. How and to what extent do you 'glorify' God?

Day 30

OBEDIENCE *in a*

SPIRITUAL BATTLE

2 Corinthians 10:1–6

Paul's tone now changes sharply, leading scholars to speculate about whether chapters 10–13 originally belonged here (see the Introduction). But Paul was quite capable of quickly 'changing gears' for one reason or another when he dictated his letters (compare the break between Philippians 2 and 3); we have already seen something of that in 6:14–7:1. Throughout the letter he's encouraged the Corinthians and accented the positive, but he's also shown awareness that his leadership is being criticized on many counts in Corinth (see 1:12–14, 17, 23–24; 2:17; 3:1; 4:2; 5:11–13; 6:3; 7:2; 8:20). Paul at last turns to address directly the fundamental challenge to his authority caused by 'false apostles' (11:13), intruders from outside the church.

He begins with what amounts to a call for obedience (10:1–6). But notice how he does it. His starting point is the character of Jesus (10:1a). The word translated 'meekness' (*prautes*; see Matthew 5:5; 11:29) doesn't mean softness or timidity, but an attitude of submission to God, or 'strength under control' (William Barclay). It's the opposite of acting harshly out of self-interest (as did his opponents; 11:20–21). Gentleness (*epieikeia*) isn't softness, but gracious forbearance, instead of insisting on the letter of the law. Paul knew about the character of Christ, and he sought to act by the Spirit in that same spirit.

Meekness and gentleness don't prevent Paul from speaking with strong irony. The words 'I who am humble...' echo a charge against him from his opponents (see 10:10). Although he had threatened to discipline some church members in 1 Corinthians 4:18–21, he hadn't done so when he was slandered by the offending brother on Paul's second visit to Corinth. His reticence to discipline the man on the spot apparently caused those who would be quick to wield power to accuse him of cowardice (see 11:20f). The irony is that Paul wasn't 'servile' (one meaning of the Greek word 'humble'), but exhibiting the humility of Christ, something his arrogant opponents sadly lacked. He's asking the congregation to respond in such a way that he won't have to confront them with the same boldness he will have when he 'dares' (and he will!) to confront his critics (10:1b).

Paul has no desire for conflict, although sometimes he had to confront. Some in Corinth were saying that he was ineffective and acting 'according to human standards' (literally, 'according to the flesh'), instead of by the power of the Spirit (10:2; see 1:17). Unlike his opponents, he doesn't typically boast about his visions, revelations, signs and wonders, all of which the Corinthians saw as signs of the Spirit's power (12:1, 11–12).

In 10:3–6 Paul uses military imagery to show that he doesn't shrink from spiritual 'warfare'. Picking up his opponents' language, he says that although he lives 'in the flesh' (that is, as a human being), he doesn't fight that way (10:3). He has powerful, divine weapons that are thoroughly effective (10:4). From what Paul says elsewhere we can expect those weapons to include the gospel itself (God's power to deliver people, Romans 1:16), the Holy Spirit, faith, love, hope, truth, righteousness and more (1 Thessalonians 5:8; Ephesians 6:14–17; 2 Corinthians 6:6–7).

This kind of spiritual armoury equips Paul for the battle that matters most. Ancient cities often had a heavily fortified command centre which became their last stronghold of defence if the walls collapsed. Paul is able to bring down 'strongholds' in which others trust, with God's wisdom—the message of Christ crucified (10:4; see Proverbs 21:22; 1 Corinthians 1:18, 24; 2:5). He brings down (a more literal translation than 'destroy') rationalizations and high-minded notions and attitudes that block the way to people coming to know God (10:4b–5a). Much of Paul's ministry has been spent in showing from the scriptures how the Messiah had to suffer and die as Jesus did (see Acts 17:2–3), and in seeking to display the same character as his Lord. His goal is to take captive every thought (not only his own, but the arguments of those who deny Christ) for obedience to Jesus (10:5b). Knowing that one day every knee will bow to Christ (Philippians 2:9–11), he doesn't hesitate to carry out a divinely-enabled offensive to proclaim and defend the truth of the gospel.

Paul is therefore fully prepared to deal with disobedience to the gospel among the saints. But he calls the Corinthians to full obedience first, because he doesn't want to have to discipline them (by expulsion from the community) as he will the intruders who continue to oppose him. Everything is at stake. If all of the congregation don't side with him, a showdown with his opponents could either split the church or cause everyone to abandon Paul's leadership.

Questions for thought

1. Do you know anyone who 'fights spiritual battles' in a meek and gentle spirit?

2. How important is it for Christians to be able to offer a rational defence of the gospel?

3. How well-prepared are you for the sort of spiritual battle Paul describes?

Day 31

PERCEPTIONS of POWER

2 Corinthians 10:7–11

Paul now answers two criticisms from the rival preachers who are unsettling the Corinthians. They claim that he isn't really sent by Christ as they are (10:7–8), and that despite his strong letters, Paul's physical presence and speech are unimpressive and inferior (10:9–11).

The first sentence in verse seven could be translated as a command (NRSV), a question (AV), or a statement (NIV). Paul's words in 3:1–3 and his use of the verb elsewhere favour a command. He's telling his hearers to take another look at the situation. He could simply be saying, 'We are Christians as much as anyone else,' but that's not in question here. The issue is his *authority*, as compared to that of the false apostles. The Greek text says literally, 'If anyone is confident that he is Christ's', the singular perhaps indicating that Paul is thinking of the leader of the opposition.

Paul's opponents apparently claimed to have some kind of closer link to Christ than Paul had (reflected again in his defence in 11:23). Perhaps one or more of them knew Jesus before his crucifixion. Often during the course of his ministry people questioned Paul's legitimacy as an apostle, comparing him unfavourably with the disciples who had seen the Lord. Possibly they emphasized that one sign of an apostle was being supported completely by their hearers, as Jesus had said (Luke 10:5–8)—which practice Paul had refused (1 Corinthians 9:12–18). So when he insisted on supporting himself, he opened himself up to the charge of depending upon himself and not acting with the authority of a true apostle (see 10:12).

Paul has authority but he doesn't want to have to appeal directly to it. Power is something that belongs ultimately to God, and Paul has no personal need to wield it to prove himself to anyone. But as we shall see, in a proud culture that valued boasting about accomplishments as a way of establishing status, Paul's hesitation to exalt himself has worked against him. Referring to himself as a slave (4:5) and refusing support didn't impress people who placed a high value on appearance. Although he has ambivalent feelings about doing so (10:8), he will go on to 'boast' in an ironic way in chapters 11–12 in order to show that he is not inferior to the intruders.

Unlike his opponents' use of power, his authority is for building the Corinthians up, rather than tearing them down (10:8; see also 13:10 and Jeremiah 1:10; 24:6). His word for 'tearing down' is the same found in 10:4; he will gladly tear down false arguments, but not people. Paul often uses the language of 'edification' or 'upbuilding' (see 12:19). That constructive concern governs the use of spiritual gifts (1 Corinthians 14:3, 5, 12, 26; Ephesians 4:12) and other aspects of Christian behaviour (Romans 14:19; 15:2; Ephesians 4:16). Although some today think of 'edification' as an individual concern, Paul sees it fundamentally as a corporate task, as he labours with God to build the living temple that is Christ's church. By contrast, his rivals are undermining Paul's efforts and leading his congregation astray (11:1–4).

Paul isn't ashamed of his authority, but he doesn't want to use it to terrify (the verb is stronger than 'frighten') his readers with his letters (10:9). Although the 'severe letter' no doubt included warnings, Paul doesn't seek to build his own reputation through intimidation; his goal is to motivate people to live in the truth.

Verse 10 is a quotation from the opposition, and may be quoting the leader ('they say' is literally 'he says'; 10:11 and 11:4 are also singular). In any case, it gives us one of the few bits of information we have about Paul's physical appearance. His physique wasn't impressive. This agrees with a description we have of him from the *Acts of Paul and Thecla*, written about a century later, which describes Paul as 'a man small of stature, with a bald head and crooked legs, in a good state of body, with eyebrows meeting and nose somewhat hooked, full of friendliness'. The 'weakness' could also refer to ill health, perhaps related to his 'thorn in the flesh' (12:7).

As a speaker, Paul was no orator. For those accustomed to powerful, entertaining rhetoric, his manner invited ridicule. The commentator Ernest Best observes, 'If his letters are anything to go by, his grammar went to pieces under stress.' Paul certainly shows rhetorical skill in his letters, but he was determined not to try to persuade people with style but with substance (1 Corinthians 2:1–5).

Paul's opponents need to bear in mind that there will be no inconsistency between what he says and does when he comes (10:11). Although he chooses not to impose his will on people as they do, he will certainly carry out his threat.

Questions for thought

1. The rival leaders probably believed they were doing the right thing. What can people do today to prevent the kind of antagonism between professing Christians that developed in Paul's situation?

2. 'You can't judge a book by its cover,' but people do. Where and how is personal appearance important in the life of your church?

3. How important is it for Christian leaders to exercise authority in order to be respected?

Day 32

MINISTRY WITHIN LIMITS

2 Corinthians 10:12—18

Paul has defended himself in 10:7—11; now he goes on the offensive. In 10:12 he attacks the arrogance of his opponents. In 10:13—16 he asserts his own determination to exercise his authority within the limits set by God, in contrast to the intruders who have 'invaded the pitch' at Corinth. Finally, in 10:17—18 he rebukes their boasting and self-commendation with an echo of the prophet Jeremiah's teaching and a reminder that *God's* approval is ultimately what matters.

Popular teachers of rhetoric in his day often sought to attract pupils by comparing themselves with other teachers to demonstrate their superiority. Paul refuses to play that game. But his rivals in Corinth are commending themselves (in contrast to Paul: 3:1; 5:12), even going so far as to compare themselves with each other, something so foreign to the character of Jesus that they clearly lack understanding (10:12). We don't know in what respects they compared themselves (skill in speaking; power, seen in signs and wonders; their relationships with Jesus during his earthly ministry?), but their claims appealed to all the wrong instincts among the Corinthians.

In order to understand 10:13—16, we should remember that, several years earlier, Paul and the Jerusalem apostles agreed that he had divine authority to take the gospel to the Gentiles and they to the Jews (Galatians 2:1—10). Furthermore, as a matter of principle Paul was careful in his ministry not to interfere in existing churches which were founded by others (Romans 15:20). He was content to stay within the limits God set for him. The word translated 'field' in 10:13 and 'sphere of action' in 10:15—16 (NRSV) is *kanon*, from which we get our word 'canon'. It can mean a *standard* by which something is measured, as the canon of scripture is a standard for Christians, or the *area* governed by a standard. Paul intends the latter here.

Since no one had preached the message of Christ in Corinth before he arrived, nothing was improper about Paul establishing and building up the congregation there (10:14). But rather than respecting his 'jurisdiction' as an apostle, his opponents are interfering and apparently even challenging his right to minister there. By implication, they are proudly claiming authority over the Corinthians, the 'field' that Paul and his companions have planted and watered (10:15a, 16b; 1 Corinthians 3:5–9).

Paul looks forward to a time when the Corinthians' faith will increase so that his area of ministry can expand (10:15b). By this he means that when the Corinthians 'grow up' and the current crisis is sorted out, he hopes that they will become a base of support for taking the gospel further west (10:16a). Paul ultimately wants to preach Christ as far as Spain (Romans 15:23, 28), but not in the intrusive, meddling and arrogant way of his opponents (10:16b).

Here and elsewhere in the letter Paul acknowledges that there is legitimate ground for 'boasting' (sometimes translated as 'exulting' or 'rejoicing'). He is justly proud, but it is a pride within appropriate limits, and a boasting in what the Lord has accomplished (see Romans 15:17–18; Acts 14:27). In 10:17 he summarizes Jeremiah 9:23–24, just as he has done earlier in 1 Corinthians 1:31. The fact that Paul has to repeat this verse speaks volumes about the pride of the Corinthians, who are being wowed by people who commend themselves. At the end of the day, what matters is not the praise we give ourselves nor the praise others give us, but God's applause.

Questions for thought

1. In what ways are people tempted to compare themselves with others in the Church today? Why do you think they do so?

2. Do Christians today overstep geographical or cultural limits and trespass into others' territory 'for the sake of the gospel'? If so, how?

3. Should Christians be in the business of planting new churches (even on their own territory), or should that energy be focused on building up existing ones?

Day 33

A JEALOUS APOSTLE

2 *Corinthians* 11:1–6

As the commentator C. K. Barrett observes, Paul felt that being a fool for Christ sometimes meant answering a fool according to his folly. His opponents lacked understanding when they commended themselves (10:12), but the Corinthians were listening to them. Although he has just spoken against self-commendation, Paul feels compelled to engage in some of that foolishness of boasting, in order to get through to his hearers —an indication of his desperation (11:1; see 12:11). Reluctantly, he begins a section that continues through to 12:13. The second sentence in 11:1 could be translated as a statement that his readers are already bearing with him (so the NIV), but most scholars agree that a plea makes better sense here.

Paul gives three reasons why they should bear with the 'nonsense' that will follow. First, as the Corinthians' spiritual father, he feels a certain jealousy towards them, not selfish but for God (11:2). In the ancient Near East, parents arranged their children's marriages. It was the responsibility of the father of the bride to ensure the virginity of his daughter from the day of her betrothal (formal engagement) to the day of her marriage. Paul feels a similar responsibility to keep the church, the 'bride' of Christ, pure and free from spiritual unfaithfulness until she is presented to Jesus the 'groom' when he returns (see Ephesians. 5:25–27).

But now Paul's opponents are threatening to mislead the Corinthian church away from her husband-to-be (11:3). Just as, in the Genesis story, the crafty serpent completely misled Eve (Genesis 3:1–6), so the intruders offer persuasive arguments promising much but delivering ruin. Paul's fear for his friends in Corinth is real and strong.

A second reason for Paul's plea for them to bear with him appears in 11:4. Not only are there tempters on the scene, but the Corinthians are easily tempted. In fact they've already been duped before, as the Greek construction Paul uses makes clear. The Corinthians readily put up with (the word translated 'submit to' in the NRSV is the same verb translated 'bear with' in 11:1) one who preaches another Jesus, a different spirit from the Holy Spirit, and a different gospel from that preached by Paul. Exactly what these phrases refer to is unclear, but reading between the lines of the letters we possess, we can guess.

It's doubtful that the intruders were preaching that the Corinthians needed to become Jews, otherwise Paul's response would have been similar to that in his letter to the Galatians. Had they preached blatant untruths, Paul would have tackled them theologically. But sometimes preaching only half the truth, or subtly encouraging division when preaching even the 'full truth', can be just as deadly. From 1 Corinthians we know that the church was susceptible to a triumphalist message, emphasizing the dramatic wonder-working power of the Spirit while minimizing the cross (1 Corinthians 2:1–5; and chapters 12–14). We also know that, like many Christians today in the West, the Corinthians fell into the trap of 'the cult of the personality', focusing on the messenger instead of the message (1 Corinthians 1:10–12; 3:1–9). Like immature children, some of them were all too ready to side with the opponents against Paul and the corrective grace he had to bring to the church.

A third reason for Paul's plea for them to bear with him as he plays the fool is that he doesn't consider himself to be inferior to the 'super-apostles' (11:5–6). This is apparently Paul's own term, but exactly who is he talking about? The words 'these' (NRSV) and 'those' (NIV) do not appear in the Greek text before 'super-apostles'. This leads some scholars to distinguish them from the false teachers in 11:3–4 who have intruded, just as Paul distinguished James, Cephas (Peter) and John from the false brethren in Galatians 2:4–9. If so, Paul here could be referring to the 'pillar apostles', whom the opponents perhaps claimed had commissioned them.

It seems more likely, however, that the NRSV and NIV are right to see Paul referring here to the same false teachers he has been speaking about, who act as though they are superior to the apostle. They are Jewish and have apparently come from Palestine (see 11:22), but whether they had a close connection with the Jerusalem apostles remains unknown. In any event, Paul is confident that, although he is an amateur when it comes to speech (unlike some of his opponents), he knows very well what or, better, whom he is talking about (4:6). For the Corinthians, to deny that is to deny all that he has taught to them.

Questions for thought

1. What can Christians do to avoid being deceived like the Corinthians? How should they have responded to the intruders?

2. What opportunities for learning more about the Christian faith exist in your church? Is there an option that would help you, or that you could offer to help others grow?

3. Many today are suspicious of 'head knowledge', and value experiences of God much more. How vital are both for Christian maturity, and why?

Day 34

NO STRINGS ATTACHED

2 Corinthians 11:7—11

In ancient Greece, travelling philosophers and teachers expected and enjoyed material support from local patrons. How well they were pampered reflected publicly on the generosity of their hosts, bringing the latter honour and respect among their peers. Nevertheless, Paul sensed that to take money from his hearers could play into an unhealthy pride of patronage and would undermine the grace of the gospel (1 Corinthians 9:13–18). In Macedonia and Achaia (and possibly elsewhere), he therefore supported himself by manual labour as a tentmaker (1 Thessalonians 2:9; Acts 18:3) and refused funding from the community which he was currently serving. No one could accuse him of being in the ministry for the money (2:17).

On the other hand, when the 'super-apostles' appeared in Corinth, they accepted support. With a saying of Jesus and the practice of other Christian leaders on their side (Luke 10:7; 1 Corinthians 9:4–5), they had yet another reason to question whether Paul was a 'real' apostle. He didn't act like everyone else. Obviously Paul didn't love the Corinthians (11:11), because he had effectively given them a slap in the face by not receiving payment from them!

If we hear sarcasm in the phrase 'super-apostles', we hear irony again in 11:7. Paul certainly did nothing wrong by preaching to them without charge God's good news of the forgiveness of sins in Christ. When he gave freely (the essence of grace), he was humbling himself as Jesus did so that they might one day be exalted (see 4:12; 8:9). Ironically, the Corinthians are exalting themselves, and casting aspersions on Paul's 'humiliating' practice of manual labour. This indicates that part of the problem in Corinth involved the wealthier members of the church who could afford to be patrons.

Instead of taking money from the Corinthians while he worked with them, Paul received financial help from other churches when he needed it (11:8–9). The word translated 'robbed' in 11:8 is a strong military term meaning 'to strip bare', as a soldier might deprive a fallen enemy of his weapons. Again we see Paul's strength of feeling. He expands what he means in 11:9. The churches which supplied what he lacked no doubt included the Philippians (Philippians 1:5; 4:10, 14–18) and possibly the Thessalonians, both of which were Macedonian. He has already praised the Macedonians for their sacrificial giving (8:1–6), and here we find another instance of it. When Paul accepted money from these poorer churches, he felt he was taking what little they had. The word 'robbed' probably also reflects his view of what the intruders are doing in Corinth (see on 11:20).

Paul's motive, in money matters as well as in other areas of his life, was to serve, and not to exploit (11:8; see Mark 10:45; Romans 15:8). He is careful to avoid anything that could be seen as financially dubious, even if that means that some will misunderstand and infer that his preaching is inferior because he doesn't charge for it. Some suggest that he refused payment because it would put him in a position of indebtedness to the church, so that he might be tempted to submit to the Corinthians' control, but that is unlikely, given Paul's character. He had determined not to burden his hearers financially in the past, and he has made up his mind to continue that policy in the future (11:9). His practice is a deliberate choice. He has no intention of changing his pattern of giving freely, for it demonstrates a radical commitment to reflect the transforming grace of God 'where the rubber hits the road'—personal finances.

Paul revelled in the fact that his message was *free* (11:10; 1 Corinthians 9:15–18). If the intruders boasted in their power and rhetoric, Paul would boast that his gospel of Christ is free. It surprised people, and set him apart from other speakers who could be dismissed as being out to sell something for their own gain. The adage, 'There is no such thing as a free lunch,' is a way of expressing the almost universal opinion that there is always a catch, always strings attached to any so-called 'gift' from a stranger. Paul insisted on living in such a way that no one in all of Greece could dispute that the good news of God's grace in Christ was indeed a gift freely offered. That was not to hurt the Corinthians as the 'super-apostles' perhaps alleged, but precisely because Paul loved them (11:11).

There are few pains like the pain of seeing our best intentions and actions twisted and misconstrued by others. We can hear that anguish in Paul's oaths, 'As the truth of Christ is in me' (11:10) and 'God knows I do!' (11:11). He has done everything he can to show them by his actions the character of Jesus. But, like his Lord, Paul finds his humility and self-sacrifice being misunderstood and rejected by those he loves. Sometimes that is the lot of the Christian.

Questions for thought

1. Do you think the other Christian leaders were wrong in accepting support from those to whom they preached?

2. Was Paul inconsistent in accepting help from the poor Macedonians but not from the Corinthians? Why or why not?

3. In what practical ways can Christians today demonstrate that the message of Christ is free?

Day 35

UNMASKING *the* DECEIVERS

2 Corinthians 11:12–21a

In 11:12–21a Paul dramatically 'unmasks' the intruders for who they really are and what they are doing to the Corinthians. He does not mince words. He says what he thinks, and his language describing other leaders who profess faith in Christ is shocking. How can the man who gave us that magnificent description of love in I Corinthians 13 say what we find in this passage? Perhaps in the same way that the Old Testament prophets, John the Baptist and Jesus himself had sharp words for religious leaders whose 'ministries' were leading people to spiritual ruin. Sometimes grace comes in the form of judgment.

Verse 12 refers back to Paul's practice of not accepting support from the Corinthians. He will continue to do this because he doesn't want to give his opponents an equal footing by accepting payment like they do. If he should take money for preaching he would lose the one clear advantage over the intruders that he has from offering his gospel for free. Despite his own practice, Paul believes that legitimate apostles do have the right to be supported by those to whom they served, as Jesus taught (1 Corinthians 9:1–14). But the behaviour of his opponents has gone beyond this. Apparently, they boast in their authority, and are greedy and demanding in a manner no normal missionary would be (11:20).

Without giving their names (not naming a person in a situation like this was a way of shaming them), Paul identifies the troublemakers in 11:13–15. From what he says, it is very doubtful that these people were among the original disciples of Jesus. Perhaps they used the terms 'apostles', 'workers' and 'servants', but Paul sees them in a different light. They aren't really 'super apostles' (11:5) but *false* apostles, just as there were false prophets in the days of the Old Testament. Their work is *deceitful* since they spread the errors of a different Jesus, a different Spirit and a different gospel (11:13; see 11:4). They disguise themselves as servants of righteousness offering light, but they lead people to darkness (11:13, 15). Satan does the same (11:14); Paul is probably echoing Jewish legends of Satan appearing in the brightness of an angel to tempt Eve. By adopting the same means as the 'adversary' (the meaning of 'Satan'), the false apostles are in effect his servants, rather than Christ's as they profess to be (11:15). They will reap what they sow on judgment day (11:15; see 5:10; 1 Corinthians 3:17).

In verse 16, Paul resumes the thought he began back in 11:1. He is about to launch into a spree of 'boasting' in response to the boasting of the false apostles, so he again asks permission to do so. Although not really a fool (someone who lacks good sense like the false apostles who boast), he is prepared to act like one and boast for a little while. He knows what he is about to say is not the way the Lord would speak (11:17). But since his opponents are winning the Corinthians by their boasting, he is prepared to fight fire with fire (11:18), even if it is alien to him to act 'according to human standards' (1:17; 5:16; 10:2).

Paul's biting irony in 11:19 is similar to what we find in 1 Corinthians 4:10: 'We are fools for the sake of Christ, but you are wise in Christ.' The truth is just the reverse. They should go along with his 'foolish boasting' because they tolerate much more foolishness from his opponents. The Greek word translated 'put up with' in verses 19–20 is the same one he has used in 11:4 to describe how the Corinthians submit to the distortion of truth presented by the false apostles. Now Paul cites five more marks of the intruders which reveal that the Corinthians are enduring a foolishness far worse than his behaviour (11:20).

The troublemakers *domineer* in their use of power, enslaving the Corinthians by ordering them about (see Galatians 2:4 for the same word). Real Christianity is about setting people free in Christ, not lording it over them (1:24; see 1 Peter 5:3). Second, they *prey* upon them (the verb literally means 'to devour') like animals, with their greedy demands for support. Third, they *exploit* (literally 'taking') the church, making it their own and no doubt intending to use letters of commendation from Corinth to enable them to exploit others. Fourth, they *act superior* (the same word used in 10:5 of proud obstacles 'raised up' against the knowledge of God), just the opposite of Jesus' humility. Fifth, they *harshly discipline* (literally 'beat', here possibly referring to physical blows) the Corinthians, in contrast to the manner of Paul and his Lord. Again speaking ironically, Paul concludes that he and his companions were too 'weak' to act with the kind of authoritarian 'strength' shown by the intruders.

False prophets and apostles were such a problem in the early days of the church that the *Didache* (a collection of Christian teachings written down around the end of the first century) offers several tests to detect them. Signs of a false prophet included dependence on Christian hospitality for more than two days, ordering a meal or asking for money for themselves 'in the spirit', asking for money or more than bread when leaving for their next destination, and generally not practising what they preached (*Didache* 11:5–12).

Questions for thought

1. How can a church that rightly values and encourages diversity distinguish genuine servants of Christ from those who serve other ends?

2. What specific steps can be taken to prevent the abuse of power by Christian leaders?

3. Would you have adopted Paul's strategy here? Why or why not?

Day 36
WEAK, *and* PROUD OF IT!

2 *Corinthians* 11:21b–33

With one last acknowledgment that what he is doing is foolish, Paul finally launches fully into the boasting he has been apologizing for since 11:1 (11:21). He has the lineage of a true Jew (11:22), the experiences of suffering and deprivation fit for one who dies daily after the example of Christ (11:23–27), and the anxiety which accompanies leadership that truly loves and identifies with people (11:28–29). Though it may be hard for the Corinthians to believe, he prefers to boast of his weakness (11:30–31), a weakness epitomized in his humiliating escape from Damascus (11:32–33).

Paul begins by matching the troublemakers point by point in the area that mattered most to them—their Jewishness. He too is a Hebrew who can read and speak the ancient languages of his people, an Israelite who is one of the chosen people, and a descendent of Abraham and so an heir of the promises made to him (11:22). This he repeatedly had to assert when Jews questioned his background (see Philippians 3:4–5). But when he gets past lineage, over which he had no control, to the issue of ministry, his better instincts again tell him that boasting in his own accomplishments is crazy (11:23). He would *never* in his right mind say that he was a 'better' minister of Christ than another. That would be for God to decide (1 Corinthians 4:4–5). But his opponents who claim to be Christ's apostles (11:13) are behaving in a way totally at odds with the crucified one who invites us to take up the cross.

So instead of listing his gifts, abilities, and 'success' seen in quantity of converts—the signs many would cite as qualifications for leadership, Paul offers a catalogue of sufferings. For him, the marks of true spirituality are not found in oratory, dominance or signs and wonders, but in the pattern of Christ's dying and living revealed in the life of his apostle (see 4:10–11). In a competition based on hardships suffered for Jesus, Paul beats the intruders hands down.

His list in 11:23b–27 expands on the experiences he has already alluded to in 6:4–5. Acts 16 tells us of only one imprisonment prior to the writing of 2 Corinthians, a reminder of its selective nature. Paul had once flogged Christians (Acts 22:19); by now he has lost count of how often he himself has been beaten. But he remembers the most severe times. Deuteronomy 25:1–3 forbids more than forty lashes as a punishment, and the Jews were careful not to exceed it by miscounting (11:24). The punishment included 26 lashes to the back and 13 to the chest. The fact that Paul suffered this five times says something about his determination to take the good news of Jesus into synagogues, and confirms the general picture Luke gives us in Acts.

Three times, including once in Philippi (Acts 16:22–23), Paul was beaten by the Roman civil authorities with rods (11:25). At Lystra he was stoned and left for dead (Acts 14:19). In all, Paul endured at least *four* shipwrecks, since the only one Acts records occurred after this letter was written. Luke tells us nothing about Paul's night and day adrift in the open sea, although, according to Acts, Paul had already made at least nine or ten sea voyages when he sent 2 Corinthians.

Danger was no stranger to Paul. He uses the word eight times in 11:26 to describe the various places and people that threatened his life: flooded rivers, bandits hiding in mountain passes and along deserted stretches of road, Jews and Gentiles who found Paul's message unsettling. Wherever he went and even among professing Christians (like those with whom the Corinthians were enamoured), Paul's life was in jeopardy.

Paul also knew deprivation (11:27). As an itinerant labourer, he worked hard to support himself, and besides fasting voluntarily, he sometimes had to make do with little food and clothing. With nowhere to lay his head on his journeys, Paul slept rough many nights. The inns along Roman roads were often little more than brothels, which is why Christian hospitality was so highly prized in the early church.

Without e-mail, a telephone or even second-class post, Paul was often kept in suspense as he waited for news of the congregations he founded (11:28; see 2:13; 1 Thessalonians 3:5). A man under constant pressure, he shares Jesus' concern for people (Luke 13:34), and identifies with their hurts and struggles. When they fall, he feels their vulnerability; when others cause them to stumble, like his Lord he gets angry (11:29; Mark 9:42).

In summary, if boasting is necessary, Paul will be proud of his weakness (11:30). To a culture that prized power and strength, these words were shocking, so Paul calls God as witness that he is telling the truth (11:31). As a final proof of his weakness, he recounts the shame of his escape from Damascus in what was hardly a triumphal manner (see also Acts 9:23–25). This example of danger, humiliation, and deliverance by God's grace sums up the pattern of a life that Paul will 'boast' about, because it follows the pattern of Jesus.

Questions for thought

1. As the commentator Linda Belleville writes, Paul here lists 'what many a search committee would view as pastoral handicaps and not strengths: ministerial trials and tribulations'. How important to service is suffering?

2. Paul's 'catalogue' of hardships puts our own problems in a new perspective. What difficulties are you facing now?

3. What do you think kept Paul going?

Day 37

REVELATIONS, VISIONS &
TRUE SPIRITUALITY

2 Corinthians 12:1–7a

In this passage Paul reluctantly tells of a spiritual experience to show that he isn't deficient or inferior to the false apostles. His language in 12:1, 'I will go on to...', and his words in 12:11f suggest that the intruders boasted of their dramatic personal encounters with God. This appealed to the Corinthians, who themselves engaged in a sort of 'competition' to see who could demonstrate their spirituality in the most spectacular way (1 Corinthians 12–14). Again, although Paul would normally never engage in such 'one-upmanship', he finds himself compelled to keep on 'competing' through boasts, or else, by his silence, lose the Corinthians to his 'more spiritual' successors.

Paul too values spiritual experiences, and Luke records several visions he had during his ministry (Acts 9:12; 16:9f; 18:9f; 22:17–21; 23:11; 27:23ff), in addition to Christ's appearance to Paul on the road to Damascus (Acts 9:3ff; 22:6ff; 26:13ff). But, judging by his letters, these were experiences Paul didn't 'wear on his sleeve' in his pastoral ministry. When challenged as to his calling, Paul referred to his conversion, but otherwise if people wanted to see a sign of God's power, he pointed them to the cross or to the transforming power of the gospel. Dramatic experiences can be wonderful encouragements to a believer. And Paul, like all of us, treasured times when he sensed that God was revealing himself in a special way to him (12:7b). But if we come to depend upon such experiences, we no longer walk by faith, but by sight. Rather than building faith, they can become a crutch, or worse, an addiction.

Although Paul speaks of the one who had the vision in the third person (literally, 'I know a man...', 12:2), there is little doubt that he is referring to himself (see 12:7). A vision to someone else would give him no ground for boasting like his opponents, since he knew them too! He's trying to avoid *direct* boasts about his own visions because he doesn't wish the Corinthians to elevate him for his spiritual experiences (see also 12:6). That's precisely their problem. The last thing Paul wants is to perpetuate the mentality that evaluates others according to how many miracles they have worked or witnessed.

We would perhaps expect Paul to refer to his conversion experience, but that would play into the hands of his opponents. Paul didn't think of his Damascus road calling as a private, subjective vision, but as something just as real as Christ's post-resurrection appearances to his disciples. Instead he refers to an experience fourteen years before (about AD42), some seven to ten years after he had become a Christian and long before he ever met the Corinthians (12:2).

Twice Paul says 'the man' was 'caught up' (12:2, 4), a Greek verb he uses elsewhere only in 1 Thessalonians 4:17. We get our English word 'rapture' from the Latin translation of this term. Jewish mystics often distinguished several successive 'heavens', some three and others as many as ten. Since 12:4 specifies Paradise (see Luke 23:43; Revelation 2:7), Paul is thinking of the home of the faithful in the very presence of God—as 'high' as someone could go. There he heard things too sacred to repeat (12:4), something strikingly unusual for an apostle who normally emphasized that the 'mystery' of salvation was not hidden, but revealed for all to see in Christ. Whatever we may think today, Paul's hearers would have been familiar with this kind of language, and suitably impressed.

But what kind of experience did he have? Was he physically taken somewhere, or was it like a dream? Just like us, the Corinthians would be fascinated with details, particularly since the Greeks thought that the body is the prison of the soul (see Day 15 on 5:1–10). Paul confesses his ignorance rather than speculating (12:2b–3). He doesn't have to understand exactly *how* things happen in his relationship with God. The Maker understands the 'metaphysics', and that is good enough for Paul. Some find it unsettling to hear Christian leaders occasionally say 'we don't know'; many of us find it honest and liberating.

Although many texts in Paul's day were full of details as to what visionaries saw and heard, Paul's account is remarkably short. Having given them a glimpse of his own experience, he quickly steps back and qualifies what he is doing (12:5–7). He could boast about the Paul of fourteen years ago who had such an encounter, but he insists on boasting in his weakness instead (12:5). Again we hear Paul's ambivalence about what he is doing: if he does boast of his experiences he won't be a fool who talks nonsense, because such exceptional revelations actually happened to him (12:6a, 7). But he won't go on, because such events are ultimately far less important than how he lives in Christ (12:6b). Paul refuses to play the game of trying to make people think more of himself than what is really there to be seen and heard.

Questions for thought

1. Does a person have to talk about his or her spirituality to be a spiritual person?

2. How should a church respond to a member who declares that God has told him/her something? How can we 'test' such claims in love?

3. Why are people so hungry for direct and immediate encounters with God? Is it wrong to desire that?

Day 38

POWER *in* WEAKNESS

---

2 Corinthians 12:7b–10

This passage takes us into the engine room of Paul's spiritual life. He has just spoken of his exceptional encounters with God (12:1–7a). Now he draws a conclusion ('Therefore...', 12:7b). We might expect him to finish with triumphal confidence in God's power revealed in such visions.

But that is not the kind of power that stokes the fire in Paul's life. In fact, however thrilling his visionary experiences may have been, they have proven dangerous, because they threaten to puff Paul up with pride (12:7; like his opponents and the Corinthians). The Greek verb translated 'to keep me from becoming *conceited*' (NIV; a better translation than the NRSV's 'too elated') is used twice in 12:7 for emphasis. Paul's 'thorn' in the flesh is a preventative measure. Whatever spiritual kudos that might come from extraordinary encounters with God has been balanced by an unrelenting problem that torments Paul and keeps him humble.

The identity of Paul's 'thorn in the flesh' remains a mystery. It could refer to (1) spiritual harassment by temptation or demonic oppression ('a messenger of Satan'), (2) persecution by an individual or group, or (3) a mental or physical disability (see 10:10; scholars have suggested depression, fever, stammering, epilepsy, or eye problems—the most common guess, based on Galatians 4:13–15; 6:11). The latter is perhaps most likely, but whatever the 'thorn', it bullied Paul. The word 'torment' is literally 'to beat with the fist', and describes the beating Christ received from Roman soldiers (Mark 14:65; Matthew 26:67).

The reference to Satan has been misused to support some bad theology. Paul is certainly not referring to demonic possession, nor is he implying that all suffering is a result of

Satanic activity. Neither does Paul view the adversary as an equal opposite to God. In the New Testament as well as in the Old Testament book of Job, Satan has only the power and room to manoeuvre that God allows. Ultimately, God can turn what the adversary does to serve a better purpose. Although Paul sees Satan afflicting him in his besetting difficulty, the adversary can do so only because he is God's instrument to make Paul usable for more effective ministry.

Paul's problem did not go away. He prayed three times for relief (12:8), but the thorn remained. Some might say that Paul didn't pray enough (he probably means three prolonged seasons of prayer rather than simply three mentions of the problem), but despite strong faith, not every prayer in the New Testament received a 'yes' answer—at least not the 'yes' desired. Paul left Trophimas ill at Miletus (2 Timothy 4:20). More significantly, Paul's Lord had prayed three times in Gethsemane, yet he was crucified (Matthew 26:39–44).

Paul's prayer didn't go unanswered. Whether it came through a vision, through his recurring pain, or through the stillness of prayer, Paul heard God speak. But it wasn't the answer that a culture fixated on instant gratification would welcome. Here we find the fuel that drove Paul, and the conviction that enabled him to endure and persevere for the sake of Christ: God's grace is enough, because his power is perfected in weakness (12:9). If we could have only one verse from this letter to sum up its contents, this would be a good choice.

Instead of taking Paul out of difficulty, God gave him grace (*charis*), the gift of divine power to bear his thorn in the flesh. To remove the thorn would leave Paul unchanged and prone to boasting. To leave it and yet provide grace enabled continual transformation and conformity to the dying of Jesus (4:10–11). God's grace is sufficient, because his power comes to full strength when we are weak. It is precisely our inadequacy that opens the door for his sufficiency to work in our lives, as it did in Paul's (see 3:5–6). That truth delivers Christians from the burden of always striving to prove ourselves, as though the power in our life depends on our own resources.

It also turns Paul loose to take comfort in his trials and

explains why he is *glad* to boast in his weakness (12:9b). His weakness makes room in his life, so that Christ's power might 'take up residence' in him. The verb Paul uses here (*episkenoo*) occurs only here in the New Testament, but it is a strengthened form of the same Greek root (*skenoo*) which John uses to describe the incarnation: the Word became flesh and 'dwelt' among us. That same glory and power that tabernacled among the Israelites in the wilderness, that came to dwell in the 'weak' flesh of the person of Jesus Christ, is again shining through the weakness of Paul. That is why he can actually see something positive in the afflictions that have accompanied his ministry (12:10).

Questions for thought

1. How does this passage contribute to an understanding of 'unanswered' prayer?

2. Do you feel you have an abiding 'thorn in the flesh'? If so, is there any way that God could use that hurt to turn his power loose in your life?

3. Do you think Paul's notion of weakness fosters a morbid attitude, or one of joy? Why?

Day 39

The ECONOMICS *of* LOVE

2 *Corinthians 12:11—18*

Looking back over what he has been saying from 11:1ff, Paul sees that by boasting he has spoken like a fool (12:11). But as he said before (12:1), he has *had* to do it; in fact the Corinthians have compelled him. Because they have not defended Paul in response to his opponents' criticism, he's had to commend himself. His need to insist again that he is not at all inferior to the super-apostles (see 11:5) shows that someone has claimed just the opposite. Rather than denying his value, Paul's addition that he is 'nothing' probably echoes deliberately what his critics have said of him. He is content to be God's 'nobody' in contrast to the arrogant self-elevation of the super-apostles.

Paul has avoided speaking of the kind of signs, wonders and mighty works of spiritual power that the Corinthians have so highly prized, because he doesn't want to pander to their infatuation with outward display. Nevertheless, even in this last area he can stand toe to toe with the intruders. As well as giving him the inward power through Paul's weakness, God blessed his ministry with outward power, confirming that he is a true apostle (12:12; see Romans 15:19 and Acts 13:6–12; 14:3, 8–10; 16:16–18; 19:11f; 20:9–12; 28:1–10).

But notice that Paul chooses not to provide details, and see how carefully he qualifies his words. These signs 'were performed' (the passive verb indicating that ultimately God was producing these, not Paul), 'with utmost patience' (literally, 'with much endurance'), as he encountered opposition in his ministry. He doesn't want the Corinthians to forget that alongside the dramatic manifestations of the Spirit, the pattern of Christ's dying and rising has been played out in his life.

The Corinthians have all the evidence they need that Paul is a true apostle. In fact, the only area in which he falls behind the intruders is his reluctance to sponge off the church (12:13)! Paul returns to the issue of support already addressed in 11:7–11, anticipating that the false apostles might accuse him of treating the church worse than others by not accepting their money. With irony, he asks the Corinthians' forgiveness for not burdening them this way (see 11:9).

As he begins to contemplate his third visit to Corinth, Paul reviews his 'economic policy' towards them (12:14–18). He won't burden them because he wants them, not their money (12:14). As their spiritual 'father', he knows that parents have a basic responsibility to save funds (literally 'to treasure up') for their children. His statement that 'children ought not to lay up for their parents' isn't intended to deny the importance of honouring our parents and caring for them in later years (see Day 22 on 7:12). Paul is thinking about responsibilities with young children.

A 'consumer' mentality is so ingrained in the Corinthians that they are finding the economics of grace foreign, puzzling and suspicious, so Paul goes on. He delights in spending all that he is and has on behalf of his children (12:15; 'for you' is literally 'for your souls'). In the case of the Corinthians, that included not only his time and energy, but also his reputation, and possibly his health. Loving them more (by not taking their money) should bring a fair exchange of love. As the commentator Nigel Watson observes, 'The harshness of some of Paul's language in these last four chapters should not keep us from seeing the tenderness he still feels for these exasperating children of his' (see also 11:11).

In verses 16–18 Paul anticipates a response to what he has been saying. They may grant that he hasn't 'burdened' the Corinthians, but perhaps this policy was only a cunning ploy so that he could con them for much more, perhaps through the Jerusalem collection (12:16). Paul in effect says, 'Where is the evidence?' In 12:17 he phrases the question in such a way as to expect a 'No' answer: when he sent others to them, Paul didn't 'exploit' (the same word used in 7:2) the Corinthians through them. In particular, when Titus and the brother came to them, they didn't take advantage of the church (12:18).

What visit is Paul describing? In chapter 8 he has spoken of a future visit by Titus; those who take chapters 10–13 as a separate, later letter see Paul referring here to that trip, although Paul says *two* brothers are also coming. However, he's probably referring in 12:18 to the earlier visit of Titus mentioned in 2:12–13; 7:15–16 and intimated in 8:6 when he speaks of Titus having 'already made a beginning' in the collection there. Although 'the brother' isn't mentioned in these verses, Titus would not have travelled alone.

By bringing into the picture other brothers well known to the Corinthians, Paul shows that his integrity is just as assured as theirs (12:18b). Expecting a 'Yes' answer, he says literally, 'Didn't we walk in the same Spirit and in the same footsteps?' Unlike the different 'spirit' of the false apostles (11:4), Paul and his companions walk by the same Holy Spirit (a more likely meaning than 'spirit' referring to their attitude; see Galatians 5:16, 25; Romans 8:4) and behave in the same irreproachable manner.

Questions for thought

1. Are 'signs, wonders and miracles' more important to the founding of a church or to its continual growth?

2. A devastating criticism today is to be 'patronizing'. Is Paul guilty of this? Why or why not?

3. The culture in Paul's day assumed that parents (specifically fathers) would not only provide for their children but also save money towards their future. Is that fact relevant to the church now?

Day 40

FEARS for the FUTURE

2 Corinthians 12:19—21

At last Paul begins to wrap up his letter. But he wants the Corinthians to understand clearly why he is sending something that sounds so defensive. They shouldn't think that he's like a boxer on the ropes, or like a man on trial before them for his life (12:19; the first sentence can be translated as a question or as a statement). God is the unseen third party in whose sight Paul has been speaking. And Christ is the one who has given Paul the authority to speak, and to whom he will answer (5:10).

What the apostle has been saying all along has not been for his own benefit, but for the upbuilding of the church (see 10:8; 13:10). All of his irony and strong language in chapters 10—12 have come precisely because he loves them ('beloved'). Being a good pastor sometimes means saying what people may not like to hear. Paul isn't afraid of what the Corinthians may think of him, because he knows where he stands before God. But he does have deep concern for their future, if they don't respond to this letter (12:19–20).

Paul fears that when he comes, both he and the church will be disappointed by each other's behaviour. He doesn't want to find them disobedient to God, and they won't want to find him rebuking them in response. Paul implies here what he has said explicitly earlier: if he has to, he will act with boldness and authority towards the church (1 Corinthians 4:21) and towards his opponents (10:2, 6).

In the second half of 12:20 Paul spells out what he doesn't want to find. Although the list is similar to others in his letters (Galatians 5:19–21; Romans 1:29–31; Colossians 3:5–8) and to vice lists from Greek ethicists, Paul has good reason to believe that everything mentioned is already happening in Corinth. These are all signs that co-operation, trust and mutual support are breaking down in the church. In essence Paul fears that he will find the Corinthians abusing God's grace instead of being transformed by it.

Already there have been quarrels and jealousy between factions supporting different leaders (1 Corinthians 1:11; 3:3). 'Conceit' or 'arrogance' (literally to be 'inflated') occurs repeatedly in 1 Corinthians (4:6, 18f; 5:2; 8:1; 13:4). Paul's warnings about abuse of the Lord's supper (1 Corinthians 11:17–34), and his description of love in 1 Corinthians 13 sandwiched between chapters on the right use of spiritual gifts, indicate that people were acting selfishly, leading to disorderly worship (1 Corinthians 14:40). Boiling anger and slander certainly would have featured when they took each other to court (1 Corinthians 6:1–8); Paul himself has been slandered by some. And the notorious case of incest among them (1 Corinthians 5:1) provided something else to gossip (literally 'whisper') about. The presence of the false apostles would have intensified all these problems.

Another area of failure for the Corinthians, sexual sin, appears in 12:21. Paul uses three general terms in a progression going from bad to worse. 'Impurity' is *akatharsia*, 'uncleanness'. Similar to our word 'filthiness', it isn't limited to sexual sin but is often used with that in mind (Romans 1:24; Galatians 5:19; Colossians 3:5; Ephesians 5:3). 'Sexual immorality' translates *porneia*, part of a word group from which we derive the English term 'pornography'. Sometimes translated 'fornication', it applies to any kind of illicit sexual activity, including adultery, homosexual offences, incest and consorting with prostitutes—the last two being specific issues for the Corinthians (I Corinthians 5:1; 6:13, 18; 7:2). 'Licentiousness' is *aselgeia*, and refers to notorious public immorality and debauchery (Romans 13:13; Galatians 5:19; Ephesians 4:19). Paul isn't singling out one or two failures here; 'many' indicates a sizeable proportion of the church, and the tense of the verb translated 'previously sinned' shows that the problem was persistent.

Paul fears the humiliation of seeing his work among them undermined by moral breakdown. If he could be shamed by the Macedonians finding the Corinthians unready to give (9:4), he could be equally embarrassed before God by their finding gross immorality in the church at Corinth. Likewise, proof that Paul's gospel didn't deliver people from the bondage of sexual sin would only make conservative Jewish Christians even more critical of his law-free message. Despite living in a very pluralistic Greco-Roman culture which celebrated sexual 'liberation' (at least for males), Paul believes that God's gift of sex shouldn't be turned into a cause for shame.

Paul is more of a parent than a judge. His reaction would also include a broken heart that mourns (see I Corinthians 5:2) for those Christians who have not repented of their behaviour and who have not continued to be transformed. He understands failure and the difficulty of struggling against persistent sin (Romans 7:14–25); what would grieve him most would be to find the Corinthians refusing to grant that God called them to turn and be changed by his grace (see I Corinthians 6:11). His Lord had forgiven a woman caught in adultery; he had also told her to go and sin no more (John 8:11).

Questions for thought

1. Which of the problems Paul cites among the Corinthians gives you the most difficulty in your own life?

2. Do you think he cites sexual sins last because he thinks sex is a bad thing?

3. Why do you think people often become more angry and vocal about the misuse of sex than about violence, the misuse of money, and other sins?

Day 41

A FINAL EXAM

2 Corinthians 13:1–10

In this passage Paul gives the Corinthians a final warning (13:1–2), assures them of his ability to do what is necessary when he comes (13:3–4), calls them to self-examination (13:5), expresses his hope and prayer for their obedience (13:6–9), and summarizes his purpose in writing (13:10).

Paul has already said that this will be his third visit (12:14). He does so again here to show that he's given them a full warning, in the spirit of Deuteronomy 19:15 which he quotes in 13:1b. According to the Old Testament law, in order to make a valid charge against another it was necessary to have the evidence of two or three witnesses (see also Matthew 18:16). Paul sees his three visits fulfilling that principle.

Again he warns those caught up in *persistent* sin (indicated by the tense of the verb) and the other Corinthians (13:2). If he finds what he fears among them (12:20–21), he will not spare them ('be lenient' translates the same word used in 1:23). Paul is probably referring to expulsion from the community, what he has called being 'handed over to Satan' (1 Corinthians 5:5).

There is no grace in allowing evil to destroy the body of Christ. We should also remember that Paul has given them plenty of space and opportunity to reform, so much space that he has been criticized by others for being 'weak' and not wielding power like the false apostles (see Day 30 on 10:1–6).

Paul will not spare them, because the Corinthians literally have asked for it (13:3). Those who have questioned his authority want proof that Christ speaks through him. They will get it, but not in the way they expect. They want some dramatic miracle or spectacular display. They will see power, but it will be Christ's, not Paul's. Christ has not been 'weak' towards them, because he is already powerfully at work in them through Paul's preaching (1 Corinthians 2:4), their conversion (1 Corinthians 6:11) and in the gifts so richly given to them (1 Corinthians 1:5–7; 2 Corinthians 8:7).

Paul has boasted of his own 'weakness' because in his suffering for Christ he re-presents the mortality of Jesus. Despite Jesus' 'weakness' on the cross (itself a demonstration of power because he *chose* to suffer), he is alive, raised from the dead by God's power. Similarly, Paul his apostle shares Christ's 'weakness', his vulnerability, but he knows that ultimately he will live together with Christ in God's resurrection power (13:4). In the Greek text, the words translated by 'in dealing with you' occur at the end of the sentence. For a moment Paul has been looking far ahead to his hope of resurrection; with the addition of his final words (literally 'towards you') he snaps back to the present. That resurrection power will take the form of authority to discipline when he visits Corinth.

If the Corinthians want proof of Paul's apostleship, where is the proof that *they* are Christians (13:5)? Paul's challenge to 'test' themselves picks up the same Greek root used in 13:3 ('proof'). Self-examination can be carried to extremes, but Paul's hearers are in no danger of overdoing it! It can be healthy from time to time to take a good long look (Paul's verbs imply repeated action) at whether we too are living in the Christian faith or simply borrowing its clothes.

Paul isn't encouraging doubt, because he phrases his question about Christ being in them so as to expect a 'Yes' answer (13:5). But he knows it is possible that some who profess faith may fail the test, although he wants them all to pass (13:7–9). If they can't spot the life of Jesus in Paul and his companions, they will have trouble recognizing him in themselves.

So Paul hopes that the Corinthians will know (a more literal translation than 'find out') that he and his team do pass the test and are approved by God (13:6). We might have expected him to express hope that the church will pass its self-inspection, but the major test before them now is whether or not they recognize Christ speaking to them through Paul for their benefit. Paul prays therefore that they will not do anything evil (13:7). His prime concern is not for his reputation, but that they do what is right. What matters to him is obedience to the truth, regardless of the cost to himself (13:8). He is happy to be 'weak', if the Corinthians can thereby be truly 'strong' (13:9). So he prays that they may be *restored*. This last word is not so much 'perfect' as 'set right'; it derives from a word used of mending nets in Mark 1:19.

Summarizing what he has said, Paul states his purpose in writing (13:10). He wants his visit with them to be happy for all concerned. The Lord has given him authority for a constructive purpose rather than a destructive one (see 10:8), so if this letter has seemed severe in parts, it is in order to prevent the need for more drastic 'surgery' later.

Questions for thought

1. By what signs can a person know whether he or she is a Christian (13:5)?

2. In what sense is God 'weak' as well as strong?

3. How tolerant a person do you think Paul was?

4. Does Paul's strategy of dealing with sin in a congregation have anything to offer the church today?

Day 42

LAST & LASTING WORDS

2 Corinthians 13:11–13

People today often conclude their letters with something like, 'Say hello for me to...' or 'Give my love to...' before ending with 'Love' or some other appropriate words and their signature. Likewise, most letters in the ancient world ended in a fairly typical way. Unless we always use the same form, the way we end our letters normally reflects our mood and our basic attitude towards the recipients. The same is true for Paul's epistles.

The conclusion of 2 Corinthians is shorter than what we find in some of Paul's other letters. This could indicate worry or anxiety. On the other hand, what Paul says is warm ('brothers' would have included the 'sisters' as the NRSV translates in 13:11), and he tends to use longer endings with churches he has not visited before. Paul usually doesn't offer greetings to specific individuals in churches he knows well, perhaps because to do so would risk leaving others out.

Five exhortations in 13:11 emphasize Paul's desire to see the church move in a positive direction toward unity in love. 'Farewell' (13:11) is the usual word expressing 'goodbye' in secular Greek letters, but since it comes at the beginning of a string of exhortations, it could also be translated 'rejoice', as it normally means in Paul. The word rendered 'Put things in order' shares the same root as the word 'perfect' in 13:9, and carries the idea of restoration. Paul wants them to mend their ways and be knit together as one body in Christ.

'Listen to my appeal' translates one Greek word which could just as easily mean 'be comforted' or 'be encouraged' (see 1:4, 6; 2:7; 7:6, 7, 13 where it is used). Paul does want them to be strengthened, but this probably is a call to listen to what he has *urged* them to do, including showing love for the brother they have disciplined (2:8), being reconciled to God (5:20), not accepting the grace of God in vain (6:1), cleansing themselves from defilement (7:1), fulfilling their pledge to the collection (chs. 8–9), and recognizing his authority (chs. 10–13). 'Agree with one another' is literally 'think the same thing', meaning 'share the same attitude and goal' (see Philippians 2:2; 4:2). 'Live in peace' isn't about the pursuit of individual serenity, but about seeking to be at peace with each other in community (see Romans 12:18). The tense of this and the other four exhortations indicates that Paul sees this as an ongoing activity, rather than an overnight miracle.

The last clause in 13:11 ('and the God of love...') is more likely a comforting promise of God's enabling grace, than a result that is conditional on their fulfilling all of the previous exhortations. In Paul's theology, God doesn't abandon his people, despite what their circumstances may lead them to believe. The transformation his people are called to is not a performance based on our strength, but a life motivated and empowered by divine love and peace.

People in the ancient world often greeted each other with a kiss on the cheek, forehead or hand as a sign of friendship and respect (Luke 7:45). In Judaism, it symbolized reconciliation. The 'holy kiss' in the early church symbolized mutual forgiveness and unity of the saints ('holy ones') in Christ (13:12; see Romans 16:16; 1 Corinthians 16:20; 1 Thessalonians 5:26; 1 Peter 5:14). This may well have been something the congregation did after listening to the reading of scripture and before sharing the Lord's supper. Paul expects his letter to be read when the church gathers for worship; the 'holy kiss' will be particularly helpful after the reading of 2 Corinthians!

Although the text itself is the same, some English Bibles have thirteen verses in this chapter (NRSV), while others number 'All the saints greet you' as verse 13, and so have a total of fourteen verses (AV, NIV). In any case, this greeting is another reminder for the Corinthians that they are part of a larger unity of saints (see 1:1) which includes the Macedonian Christians with Paul as he speaks.

Many Christians know the last verse, with minor changes, by heart. 'The grace' is a magnificent prayer, summarizing the character and work of the Trinity. When we look at the life and death of Jesus we see grace in action—unconditional and generous giving to enrich others at his expense (8:9). Paul normally ends his letters with a prayer for this grace to be with all his hearers. 2 Corinthians, however, is unique in the addition of the other two members of the Trinity. Behind Christ's giving stands God's love (5:18–21; Romans 5:8) which is also poured into our hearts by the Spirit (Romans 5:5). The 'communion of the Holy Spirit' is a participation *in* the Spirit as well as a fellowship or sharing enabled *by* him. Paul gives us a model prayer, asking in confidence that the Spirit too will be at work, forming and transforming all of God's people by his grace.

Questions for thought

1. What in these last words do you think would have been most helpful to the Corinthians?

2. Is there anything equivalent to the 'holy kiss' in the life of the church today? Should there be?

3. The words of 'the grace' are often used to conclude times of prayer and services of worship. What do these words mean to you?

EPILOGUE

Looking back over the letter we know as 2 Corinthians, many features of Paul's character and ministry spring to mind:

- His concern for the effects of his words and actions on the church as a whole, as well as on its individual members.

- His anxiety for his spiritual children and his willingness to risk 'sinning boldly' by taking extraordinary steps to ensure clear communication.

- His courage to confront where necessary and to call evil evil, but always with the goal of people's reconciliation to God.

- His humanity, seen in his warmth, his fury, his pride, his elation, his passion, his enthusiasm and his discouragement.

- His sense of the splendour of Christian ministry, and his paradoxical understanding of power in weakness.

- His emphasis on giving joyfully and sacrificially.

- His determination to re-present in himself the character of Christ and his sufferings without shame.

- His reminder of holiness, and that belonging to God makes a difference in our behaviour.

- His awareness that life is lived in full view of the one before whom we will all one day give an account.

- Above all, his confidence that our great God is at work, and that his grace in Christ is sufficient to continue that transforming work already begun in his people.

If you have not done so already, perhaps now would be a good time to write down any points that have impressed you in your study of 2 Corinthians.

As he promised, Paul visited the Corinthians for a third time in the winter of AD56. Acts 20:2–3 tells us that he stayed in Greece for three months, which suggests that 2 Corinthians may have been successful. In his letter to the Romans which was sent from Corinth during that stay, Paul says that Achaia contributed to the Jerusalem collection (Romans 15:26). But forty years later, Clement the bishop of Rome needed to write to the Corinthians about some of the same issues addressed by Paul. Every generation needs to respond to the grace of God if we are to be transformers of our world rather than chameleons conformed to it.

If you have found **Transforming Grace**
helpful, you may like to try some of the
Bible Reading Fellowship's *other*
Bible guides.

New Daylight is BRF's top-selling series of daily Bible notes, written by a team of well-known and experienced authors under the guidance of Canon David Winter. Each day's Bible reading is printed out in full, together with a thought-provoking comment on the passage, and a prayer or point for reflection. The aim is to speak to both head and heart, giving readers something to ponder as they go into the day ahead.

Guidelines offers a flexible approach to daily Bible study. A team of top Bible scholars write commentaries on the passages, including information on the historical and cultural background. The commentaries are arranged in 'weeks' of about six sections which can be used daily, in a single sitting, or at the reader's convenience. Each 'week' concludes with points for thought, meditation and prayer. *Guidelines* is edited by Dr Grace Emmerson and the Revd Dr John Parr.

The People's Bible Commentary distils the best of scholarly insights into the straightforward language and devotional emphasis of Bible reading notes. It is planned to cover the whole Bible and is an invaluable resource for first-time students of the Bible, for all those who study it regularly, and anyone involved in preaching and teaching scripture. The series has three General Editors: the Revd Dr Richard Burridge, Dom Henry Wansbrough OSB and Canon David Winter.